World Trade Governance and Developing Countries

The GATT/WTO Code Committee System

Kofi Oteng Kufuor

**THE ROYAL INSTITUTE OF
INTERNATIONAL AFFAIRS**

Blackwell
Publishing

© The Royal Institute of International Affairs, 2004

The Royal Institute of International Affairs
Chatham House
10 St James's Square
London SW1Y 4LE
http://www.riia.org
(Charity Registration No: 208223)

Blackwell Publishing Ltd
350 Main Street, Malden, MA 02148-5018, USA
108 Cowley Road, Oxford OX4 1JF, UK
550 Swanston Street, Carlton South, Melbourne, Victoria 3053, Australia
Kurfürstendamm 57, 10707 Berlin, Germany

First published 2004 by Blackwell Publishing Ltd

Library of Congress Cataloging-in-Publication Data has been applied for

ISBN 1-4051-1678-1 (hardback); ISBN 1-4051-1677-3 (paperback)

A catalogue record for this title is available from the British Library.

Set in 10.5 on 13 pt Caslon with Stone Sans display
By Koinonia, Manchester
Printed and bound in the United Kingdom
by MPG Books Ltd, Bodmin, Cornwall

For further information on
Blackwell Publishing, visit our website:
http://www.blackwellpublishing.com

Contents

Contents

Acknowledgments

This study was made possible by a grant from the Nuffield Foundation. I have benefited from discussions with officials at the World Trade Organization. My findings were further enriched by comments made when an earlier version of this paper was presented to the International Economic Law Group at the British Institute of International and Comparative Law on 13 February 2001 and also to a gathering of experts at the Royal Institute of International Affairs (RIIA) on 11 October 2001. Useful feedback from Dr Brigitte Granville, Head of the International Economics Programme at Chatham House, has helped to improve this study immensely. I thank Joann Fong, the Programme Coordinator, for being so patient and understanding during the writing of this monograph. I am grateful as well to Beatrice Chaytor, Peter Holmes, Fiona Macmillan, David Ong, Sheila Page and Yvonne Apea for their suggestions and comments. However, I bear sole responsibility for the views expressed in this study.

December 2003   K.O.K.

About the author

Kofi Oteng Kufuor is a Lecturer in the School of Law, University of East London, and an Associate Fellow of the International Economics Programme at the Royal Institute of International Affairs. He was previously a Visiting Scholar at the Lauterpacht Research Centre for International Law, Cambridge University. He holds degrees from the University of Warwick, the London School of Economics and the University of Science and Technology in Ghana. He is the author of a number of articles on the WTO and the Economic Community of West African States (ECOWAS).

Acronyms

ATC	Agreement on Textiles and Clothing
BISD	Basic Instruments and Selected Documents of the GATT
CADP	Committee on Antidumping Practices
CAG	Committee on Agriculture
CAP	Common Agricultural Policy
CAMD	Committee on Avoidance of Market Disruption
CTBT	Committee on Technical Barriers to Trade
CTC	Cotton Textiles Committee
CTD	Committee on Trade and Development
CTE	Committee on Trade and Environment
DCs	Developing Countries
DSB	Dispute Settlement Body
DSU	Dispute Settlement Understanding
EC	European Community
FAO	Food and Agriculture Organization
GATT	General Agreement on Tariffs and Trade
GATS	General Agreement on Trade in Services
GEMIT	Group on Environmental Measures and International Trade
ILM	International Legal Materials
ITO	International Trade Organization
LDCs	Least Developed Countries
LTA	Long-Term Arrangement on Cotton Textiles
MERCOSUR	Common Market of the South
MFA	Multifibre Arrangement
NAFTA	North American Free Trade Agreement
NICs	Newly Industrializing Countries
NGOs	Non-Governmental Organizations
OECD	Organization for Economic Cooperation and Development

Acronyms

PCTC	Provisional Cotton Textiles Committee
PD	Prisoner's Dilemma
STA	Short-Term Arrangement on Cotton Textiles
TBT	Agreement on Technical Barriers to Trade
TC	Textiles Committee
TMB	Textiles Monitoring Body
TPRM	Trade Policy Review Mechanism
TSB	Textiles Surveillance Body
UNCTAD	United Nations Conference on Trade and Development
VERs	Voluntary Export Restraints
WTO	World Trade Organization

Introduction

The growing power and importance of the World Trade Organization[1] (WTO) marks it out for scholarly analysis.[2] The transformation of the General Agreement on Tariffs and Trade[3] (GATT) into the WTO at the end of the Uruguay Round of multilateral trade talks in 1995[4] was an ambitious attempt to constitutionalize international trade rules, institutions and decision-making.[5] The WTO's institutional framework,[6] the various agreements adopted at the end of the Uruguay Round,[7] the dispute settlement understanding[8] (DSU) and the Trade Policy Review Mechanism[9] (TPRM) serve as the pillars of its new power and importance.

The fact that the WTO's multilateral agreements are mandatory in the sense that they impose binding obligations on all its members,[10] as distinct from the practice under the old GATT whereby contracting parties could decide which agreement to adhere to, is one manifestation of its increased power. Also, the transformation of the GATT dispute settlement system, resulting in the Dispute Settlement Understanding (DSU) and the invariably binding nature of panel reports,[11] has strengthened arguments that the WTO is a supranational institution[12] with considerable authority over its members.

Reinforcing this view is the creation of the WTO Appellate Body,[13] in itself a further move away from the diplomatic underpinnings of the old GATT dispute settlement system[14] towards an emphasis on judicial power within the new WTO system. This institutional matrix has caused one observer to contend that cumulatively it will have a major impact on the national laws of the WTO's members: it will give the new 'trade constitution'[15] the kind of authority normally reserved for developed, (national) legal systems with their supervisory bureaucracies.[16]

In addition to creating the new institutions, the Marrakesh Agreement Establishing the WTO reinforces the power of the WTO by stating that all members are bound to ensure the conformity of their laws, regulations and administrative procedures with the obligations set out in the agreements.[17]

1

consequence of this, in the opinion of some supporters and critics of the WTO alike, is the creation of a global institution that challenges or undermines national sovereignty.[18] Although other scholars have argued that the WTO's threat to national sovereignty is overstated,[19] there is no doubt that the international community has created what is arguably the most powerful global institution in the post-Second World War era. In sum, the institutions for the governance of the world trading system have been transformed from the GATT, a contractual agreement between nations, to the WTO, an institution empowered to make binding rules for all its members.

The strength of the WTO as a powerful global institution gives importance to a study of its committees with particular focus on the role and impact of the developing countries (DCs). The role of the DCs in the GATT/WTO system as a whole has been the subject of much study and analysis.[20] However, there is no analysis of their involvement in the GATT/WTO committees established under the various codes and agreements.[21] This study attempts to fill that gap in the literature. The focus is on DC participation in GATT/WTO committees in the areas of antidumping, textiles, agriculture, and trade and environment. These are the most contentious areas of international trade. Antidumping actions in both DC and developed-country members of the WTO are one of the biggest threats to DC exports.[22]

The WTO has noted that trade defence measures, including antidumping actions, have continued to rise since 1995.[23] The number of antidumping investigations notified by its members to the WTO rose from 157 in 1995 to 347 in 2001.[24] This rise is partly explained by enthusiasm for this form of protection on the part of DC members of the WTO: India and Argentina were two of the four leading initiators of antidumping actions in 2001.[25] These two countries had been two of the four most enthusiastic users of antidumping investigations since 1995.[26] But the DCs are also the most often targeted with antidumping investigations, the primary subjects being China, Taiwan, South Korea, Indonesia and Thailand.[27]

Not only are antidumping actions largely inefficient, thereby generally distorting comparative advantage, but the global trade rules are also such that the DCs are more vulnerable to the negative effects of those actions. The argument is that DC export manufacturing processes rely on unskilled workers and labour-intensive processes. DC exports are subject to successful antidumping petitions because, relative to manufactures using the high-tech processes employed in developed countries, it is easier to arrive at a finding of dumping with regard to goods whose marginal costs make up a significant fraction of the price.[28]

The relative ease of finding dumping and injury is compounded by the fact that mounting a defence in an antidumping investigation can be quite costly, especially when manufacturers export comparatively small volumes of goods. Given that DCs are more likely to have such relatively smaller volumes of sales and also that the value of their exports is smaller relative to the exports of advanced countries, DC exporters are generally apprehensive about losing an antidumping investigation. Thus they are more likely to be deterred from exporting to markets where antidumping investigations are pursued regularly and vigorously.[29]

The development of a country's textile industry is seen as a precondition for its move from a mainly agrarian economy to an industrial one[30] – an aspiration long held by DCs. The Agreement on Textiles and Clothing (ATC) is intended eventually to extinguish itself, which presumably means the dissolution of its committees. But given that textile committees are among the oldest in the GATT/WTO system, an analysis of the dynamics of DC participation in them can only enrich our understanding of the impact of the DCs on the GATT/WTO system as a whole.

The DCs have a particular interest in the international trade in agricultural products, as this is another area where they have a comparative advantage over most of the developed-country members of the WTO. About 25 DCs rely on primary products for more that 50 per cent of their exports. Agricultural subsidies that depress the prices of primary commodities in overseas markets retard the economic growth of DCs. Thus the liberalization of world agricultural markets is of considerable importance to them.[31] The DCs are uncertain about the future of the international trade in this sector as they feel that the WTO's rules on agriculture still help to create barriers to their entry into the markets of the advanced countries. However, some DCs are fearful of further liberalization of the trade in agricultural products because of limitations of understanding on the part of their decision-makers and trade negotiators, particularly about how world agricultural markets function and about agricultural market trends and export opportunities. As a result, some DCs are reluctant to commit themselves fully to open agricultural markets.[32]

The importance of participation by DCs in the WTO Committee on Agriculture (WTO CAG) is reinforced further by the fact that developed countries are not the only WTO members to have erected barriers to agricultural exports. Barriers to markets in other DCs, such as bound agricultural tariffs, are considerably higher, on average, than in developed countries.[33] This seems to have been overlooked in the frequent complaints made by DCs about tariffs in advanced countries.[34]

The WTO Committee on Trade and Environment (WTO CTE) is also of importance to the DCs in view of their conviction that linking international trade rules to the need to protect the environment is a protectionist ploy by the developed countries.[35] The DCs argue that the differences between their environmental laws and those of the advanced countries are a reflection of their different stages of socio-economic development. In addition, trade sanctions aimed at improving environmental laws and practices would only retard the DCs' economic growth. They take the position that there is a link between economic prosperity (brought about in part by the benefits of open markets) and environmental protection, and thus that when they reach certain income levels their societies will press for stronger national environmental regimes. Therefore, in their view, any attempts by the advanced countries to improve DC environmental standards through the use or threat of trade sanctions flies in the face of reality and is just another protectionist tactic disguised as environmental protection.

STRUCTURE OF THE BOOK

Chapter 1 discusses international institutions, their functions and why they are of increasing significance in the GATT/WTO system. Chapter 2 evaluates the role of the DCs in the committees under the GATT, and their impact on them. Chapter 3 explores the global shift towards trade liberalization and how this development has affected DCs' attitudes towards the GATT/WTO committees. The DCs' role in the committees established under the WTO is examined in Chapter 4, and Chapter 5 assesses how the DCs' participation in the WTO committees can be improved.

The questions posed in this study are as follows: what impact have the DCs had on the GATT/WTO committees? Does the fact that DCs were late entrants into the GATT system mean that they had no or a very minimal impact on the GATT committees? How have the DCs tried to use the WTO committees? Have they had any successes? Have the WTO committees been designed to take into account the concerns of the DCs? What are the main issues the DCs have put before the committees? What is the nature of solidarity among DCs within the committees? How have factors external to the committees shaped DC participation? What are the likely implications of the DCs' increasing reliance on the WTO DSU for their participation in the committees?

To attempt to answer these questions, the study examines the interplay of relationships within the committees between developed countries and DCs and among the DCs, as well as the context within which the committees have had to operate, specifically the changing nature of international economic and political relations and trends in the global economy.

1

The importance of international law and institutions for the world trading system

INTRODUCTION

Scholarly positions on the role of international trade law and institutions are grouped into three separate categories. One perspective sees law and institutions as rather inconsequential in the design of the world trade system. This position is rooted in the Realist perspective on international relations.[1] For Realists, the international system is anarchical, characterized by conflict between states[2] and within it the state is the primary actor. This anarchy fosters competition and conflict and inhibits states' willingness to cooperate even when they share common interests. Acting rationally, the state aims to maximize its power in the international system. Thus Realists see international law and institutions both as tools of the most powerful states and as having a minimal impact on interstate relations. From their perspective, although states negotiate international agreements and establish international institutions, it is not the laws and institutions that compel them to comply with their international obligations, as there is no tendency towards world government. Rather, compliance with international law is at the discretion of the state.

A second outlook on the role of law and institutions in international trade derives from the Institutionalist perspective. Institutionalists propose that the international anarchy that Realists believe can be dealt with only through the use of state power can in fact be mitigated if states create regimes, that is 'rules, norms, principles and decision-making procedures'.[3] Regimes establish a framework within which actors in the international system can pursue their common and welfare-enhancing goals. Regimes reduce transaction costs and promote interstate and intrastate cooperation. Thus, with particular reference to international trade, regimes create the framework needed for multilateral negotiations; they legitimize state action and allow for links on issues within regimes and between regimes. In addition, international regimes play a role in supplying information to regime participants regarding the behaviour of other governments. This information enhances compliance by all with international law. Regimes also reduce states' tendency to cheat on their international obligations because they set standards that states can follow and create monitoring mechanisms to ascertain whether states are in compliance with their obligations.[4]

Thus, the major difference between Institutionalists and Realists is over the role that international institutions can and do play. Although Institutionalists agree that states are the primary actors in international relations and that without institutions states engage in the unrestricted pursuit of power, they argue nonetheless that institutions mitigate international anarchy.[5]

Liberalism, our third perspective, as applied to international relations, is the main alternative to Realist and Institutionalist theories of international relations. Liberalism has as its core two assumptions: that the fundamental actors in international politics are individuals and private groups,[6] and that these actors organize within the state in order to further their own interests. Liberal theory thus presumes that international law proceeds from the 'bottom up': political action and outcomes are 'embedded in domestic and transnational civil society'.[7]

For Liberals, the role of private interests signifies that the state is not an opaque, unitary actor as argued by the Realist school.[8] Rather, it is an arena for repeated competition between interest groups. Thus, a state's foreign policy is determined by coalitions of domestic and transnational interest groups.[9] In view of the anarchy of the international system,[10] Liberals argue that international cooperation can be greatly enhanced if transnational processes create a pattern of benefits and costs conducive to the formation of common interests among states.[11]

Liberals therefore see international trade law and institutions as important because, notwithstanding the welfare-enhancing effects of international trade,[12] there is an incentive for governments to renege on their international trade obligations and commitments. The essence of this behaviour is captured in the two-player game theory scenario known as the Prisoner's Dilemma (PD).[13] In the PD, players act solely to advance their own interests. Thus, a state will avoid its obligations if that yields a higher dividend or payoff than cooperation.

In international trade, however, avoidance of obligations lowers the welfare of all states in the PD game in the long run, and compliance with the rules of the game yields welfare-enhancing dividends. As a result of the current economic interdependence of states, protectionist measures, i.e. a player's breach of the rules of the international trading system, cause harm not only to that player but also to its trading partners. The consequences of protection are aggravated even further should all participants in an international trade system choose to impose barriers to trade.

In the Liberal construct, the role of international law and institutions is to constrain to the extent possible any protectionist inclinations of states. Constraints are imposed on protectionist behaviour through the creation and maintenance of international institutions for the governance of trading relations. Such institutions allow for communication between the parties to a trade agreement and thus reduce the incentives to avoid one's obligations.[14]

Adherents to Liberal theory adopt a range of approaches for understanding the role of international law and institutions, among them analysing the decision-making process of institutions and examining how institutional relations influence the evolution of national and international trade policies. In examining the role of DCs[15] in GATT/WTO code committees and their impact on them, I draw on those approaches and focus on how decision-making processes[16] operate within committees and on the committees' institutional evolution and dynamics, and their consequences for the DCs.[17]

THE INSTITUTIONAL STRUCTURE OF THE GATT/WTO SYSTEM

At the apex of the GATT/WTO system is the Ministerial Conference. It meets at least every two years, comprises all the WTO's members and carries out the functions of the WTO. The next institution in the hierarchy is the General Council of the WTO, which consists of all the WTO's members and carries out the functions of the Ministerial Conference in the intervals between the latter's meetings. When appropriate, the General Council converts itself into the Dispute Settlement Body or the Trade Policy Review Body.[18]

There are three councils beneath the General Council: the Council for Trade in Goods, the Council for Trade in Services, and the Council for Trade-Related Aspects of Intellectual Property Rights, each of which reports to the General Council. They oversee the functioning of the Agreement on Trade in Goods, the Agreement on Trade in Services and the Agreement on Trade-Related Aspects of Intellectual Property Rights respectively, and carry out the functions assigned by these agreements and the General Council.

The General Council is also authorized to establish working parties to study important issues as they arise. Working parties comprise any interested contracting party and, together with the committees, play an extremely important role. National delegations work together to submit recommendations, reports or conclusions to the General Council or the contracting parties. Thus, a large part of the negotiation and conciliation of national interests occurs at the level of the committees and the working parties.[19]

A range of committees, each with its mandate and membership, makes up a further part of the GATT/WTO institutional set-up. Some are standing committees whose contracting parties consult with each other on matters within a committee's remit. Then there are committees on trade negotiations, whose purpose is to oversee periodic trade talks.[20] Finally, a third group consists of committees established under the codes and agreements negotiated during the Tokyo Round of trade talks and also as a consequence of the regulation of the trade in textiles and clothing.[21] This last group of committees is the subject of analysis in this study.

THE ROLE OF INTERNATIONAL TRADE INSTITUTIONS

It has been noted above that, in international relations, institutions are deemed important by proponents of Institutionalism and Liberalism because of the complexities of the international system and the lack of a central power or body akin to the executive arm of a national government that can enforce the rule of law.[22] Beth Yarbrough and Robert Yarbrough have applied Ronald Coase's analysis of transaction costs[23] to explain the creation of international institutions.[24] They assert that the potential for opportunism exists in international relations because of the lack of restraints on state action.[25] As a result, effective international governance of international transactions may require a range of institutions to mitigate the perverse consequences of the lack of an international sovereign authority.

A second rationale for international institutions is that they can be used to pursue policy-makers' redistributive goals. In effect, institutions can serve as mechanisms by which interests pursue their objectives,[26] and this applies to international committees as well.[27] For example, the DCs managed to persuade the GATT contracting parties to establish the Committee on Trade and Development (CTD) as the institutional arm of Part IV of the GATT, which is intended to secure trade policies that are favourable to less-developed-country (LDC) contracting parties.[28] The CTD has a range of functions relating to the workings of Part IV.[29]

International institutions play a third role: they serve to limit or to prevent government failure. An example of government failure is protectionism,[30] usually the result of deliberate government policy.[31] Domestic import-competing lobbies use a variety of strategies in the form of legislation and regulations to secure protection from law-makers and other public officials.[32] In international economic relations this protection takes the form of policy tools such as antidumping investigations, safeguard actions and countervailing duties. It is to prevent or at least mitigate the impact of protectionism that, for example under the WTO Agreement on Safeguards,[33] the role of the Committee on Safeguards[34] is to conduct surveillance on the implementation of the Agreement on Safeguards, to determine whether the procedural requirements relating to the adoption of a safeguard measure under the agreement has been complied with, to monitor the phase-out of certain safeguard measures, to review suspended concessions or other obligations taken by members, and to receive and review all safeguard notifications under the agreement.

There is similar provision for the Committee on Subsidies and Countervailing Measures under the WTO Agreement on Subsidies and Countervailing Measures.[35] This committee reviews matters referred to it by members of the WTO concerning subsidy programmes of other members that may have a serious adverse impact on the complaining members' economies.[36] Thus, this committee and the Committee on Safeguards serve as institutions created to counter the trade-restricting impact of government protectionism.

The assumptions of relational contract theory reinforce the importance of institutions for world trade. The premise of relational contract theory is that commercial exchange is hardly ever 'arm's-length bargaining' between two or more unrelated parties. Instead, contractual relations are normally subsumed within the context of continuing relationships between the parties to a contract.[37] As is the case with most contractual relations, parties usually have to deal with the hazards of opportunism,[38] their bounded rationality and that of the other parties to the bargain[39] and the changing context within which the contract was initially agreed. These stumbling blocks to fruitful contractual arrangements are more formidable when the parties are states trading in an international setting in which, as noted above, there is no world executive authority similar to that of a national government.

For this reason, long-term contractual arrangements tend to regard governance mechanisms as extremely important and to build them into contracts so as to allow parties, in our case members of the WTO, to deal with unforeseen circumstances arising from their treaty obligations. Without institutions for this purpose, the parties to an international agreement may refuse to enter into the contract in the first place. It is in this context, then, that we can understand the roles played by WTO committees in authorizing and monitoring departures by members from their agreed obligations and commitments. Thus, institutions serve to reduce collective action problems, especially the commitment and enforcement problems that so tend to undermine international relations.[40]

Another role of international institutions is that they have the potential to socialize their participants. Participation in the work of WTO committees can shape the outlook of DC trade representatives. This is the role of committees as 'transformative institutions', arenas for the analysis and discussion of trade issues which can also shape the thinking of the participants.[41] This process induces allegiance to the WTO system in this case and thereby enhances the stability of the WTO system, which is in the interests of the DCs.[42] In addition, national trade representatives who have participated at length in committee deliberations can, on return to their home countries and their reintegration into the national bureaucracy, serve as 'agents' for the socialization of national civil servants who are hostile to the WTO.[43]

2

Developing countries in the GATT committee system prior to the establishment of the WTO

INTRODUCTION

DC participation in the GATT/WTO committee system has been shaped by two main factors. First, there is the self-interest rationale. It has become obvious that the DCs could benefit from participating in the workings of the committees. As noted previously, GATT/WTO committees have served (and continue to serve) as mechanisms to restrain protectionism. Hence non-participation by DCs with an increasing stake in the opening up of the global trade system would be self-injurious. It could well result in the developed countries seizing control of committee agendas and shaping deliberations and conclusions to suit their interests.[1]

Second, given the supposed complexity of GATT/WTO issues, participation in committee deliberations can help the DCs to understand those issues. The GATT/WTO system has developed from a rudimentary form in the late 1940s into a complex and technical matrix of codes and jurisprudence.[2] As most of the DCs are relative newcomers to this system, there is a steep learning curve for them. The committees, with their discussion of code provisions and the role some of them still have in the settlement of disputes, are therefore valuable forums for understanding how the global trade system functions.[3]

THE GATT COMMITTEES ON ANTIDUMPING PRACTICE

Dumping has long been a problematic issue in world trade.[4] For this reason, the GATT contracting parties stated that dumping was to be condemned if it injured world trade.[5] But, realizing that domestic import-competing interests could exploit antidumping actions and thus frustrate the objective of an open trading system, the GATT adopted the Antidumping Code in 1967, reproduced, partly, in the Appendix.[6] The Code created the Committee on Antidumping Practices[7] (from here on the 1967 CADP).

The 1967 CADP was mainly a consultative forum. Its primary role was that parties to the Antidumping Code could use it to discuss matters relating to the administration of their antidumping systems.[8] However, none of the DCs signed the Code,[9] and with the exception of its 1971 meeting, where the 1967 CADP did note the problems of DCs adhering to the Code,[10] there is no evidence that issues of concern to DCs were given any serious consideration in its early deliberations.

Even so, the non-participation of DCs in GATT antidumping issues did have an indirect impact on the work of the 1967 CADP. In the absence of DCs, it became a forum for GATT contracting parties with largely similar levels of economic development.[11] In such a homogeneous committee, there was a tendency to avoid litigation as a means of settling intra-group disputes.[12] In effect, the 1967 CADP was a largely cohesive group, and this is a probable additional reason why it was not accorded any formal dispute-resolution powers. Moreover, non-participation by DCs made it very easy for the developed countries to design the 1967 CADP as a talking shop, free from the North–South tensions[13] that active DC involvement most probably would have created.

This point on the indirect impact of the DCs on the 1967 CADP is supported by the nature of the DC participation in and impact on the 1979 CADP.[14] By the end of the Tokyo Round, the attitudes of the DCs towards the GATT had started to change.[15] In the later stages of its existence, the 1967 CADP had begun to be influenced by the DCs, and issues of concern to them were placed before it by Egypt in 1978. The DCs stressed that conditions in their home markets compounded their unfair treatment by the developed countries. They pointed out that there were structural imbalances in their economies, a consequence of their underdeveloped state. These imbalances, reflected in their technological inadequacies, the poor state of their transport infrastructure, weak marketing and distribution services and balance-of-payments problems, led to high prices of domestically produced goods.[16] Thus, DCs' home market prices were usually above prices in developed-country home markets.

In effect, this was unintentional or unavoidable price discrimination between markets, but it still led to findings of dumping against the developing countries. As products from developing countries had to meet the 'world price' in the developed countries if they were to achieve export sales, the disparity was said to lead to artificial findings of dumping against developing countries because the 'normal value' in developing countries was artificially high. The DCs thus requested that their home market conditions be taken into account whenever the advanced countries launched antidumping investigations.[17]

However, the 1967 CADP, still the preserve of the advanced countries, refused to grant the DCs their request. Why was this request turned down? My contention is that at the time the only GATT-agreed definition of dumping was price discrimination between markets. If DCs' exports were not held up to this provision because of domestic 'special circumstances', then it was probable that none of them would be in breach of the 1967 Anti-dumping Code. This implied opening the door further to a flood of cheap exports at a time when the rise in oil prices in the 1970s had caused severe shocks to the economies of the advanced countries. With their economies in recession as a consequence, the last thing the main instigators of anti-dumping investigations wanted was to allow the newly industrializing countries (NICs), in particular, to avoid being sanctioned for dumping cheap manufactured goods in their markets.

It was only with the conclusion of the 1979 Antidumping Code that the developed countries granted the DCs their request. This was because the 1979 Antidumping Code broadened the definition of dumping to include less than fair-value sales.[18] Compared to ascertaining whether there was price discrimination between markets, the below-cost-sales approach was highly complex. This was in part because of the large number of adjustments that national investigating authorities were allowed to make in arriving at their conclusions about whether dumping (and injury) had taken place.[19] Now the developed countries could be generous in their handling of the DCs' request for special consideration of their home market prices: not only was there an additional GATT-sanctioned definition of dumping but the broad discretion in the new code's provisions was also extremely useful for dealing with any threat to DCs' domestic import-competing industries.

At the end of the Tokyo Round, the contracting parties adopted a new antidumping code.[20] This established the 1979 CADP,[21] which had an increased range of functions compared to its predecessor. In addition to fulfilling its consultative role,[22] the 1979 CADP was to receive reports on preliminary or final antidumping actions taken by the parties to the Agreement,[23] to receive semi-annual reports from the parties on any antidumping actions taken within the preceding six months[24] and to play a role in resolving antidumping disputes.[25] This was in contrast to the relatively softer language of the 1967 Code, which did not specify to whom the parties should send information on changes in their antidumping laws and regulations.[26] The 1967 Code also did not mention who should receive information on the administration of the signatories' antidumping laws and any antidumping duties they imposed.[27]

The greater powers of the 1979 CADP reflected the DCs' emerging interest in the GATT antidumping system. First, the 1979 CADP had the discretion to consult with 'appropriate sources' in furtherance of its functions, and could also work with the signatories to the Code.[28] In effect, it was now authorized to develop a close working relationship with the antidumping authorities and possibly with antidumping petitioners as well. Arguably, any successful antidumping challenge to DC exports would benefit from a close working relationship with affected developed-country firms.[29] Hence, opening up the 1979 CADP to representations from private interests would enable those interests to influence its deliberations. It is not known whether there were any consultations between the 1979 CADP and any of the developed-country contracting parties' national bureaucracies or developed-country import-competing interests. However, it is possible that this provision strengthened the hand of those signatories which wished to rely on the 1979 CADP to serve the interests of their protectionist constituencies.

Second, the 1979 Antidumping Agreement elaborated on the dispute settlement role of the 1979 CADP. Until the end of the Uruguay Round, dispute settlement under the GATT was fragmented. Most of the codes negotiated during the Tokyo Round had their own dispute settlement body in the form of their respective committees.[30] Under the 1979 Antidumping Code, if any of the signatories felt that any rights accruing to the CADP under that code had been nullified or impaired or that another signatory or other signatories were impeding the achievement of any of the Code's objectives, the aggrieved signatory could initiate consultations under the Code.[31] If consultations failed to achieve a solution acceptable to all signatories involved and final antidumping duties were imposed or price undertakings were offered by the importing country, the aggrieved signatory could refer the matter to the 1979 CADP for conciliation.[32] The 1979 CADP was to meet within 30 days after a matter for conciliation had been referred to it and to encourage the parties involved to reach a mutually acceptable solution. But if the parties involved failed to reach a mutually acceptable solution, the 1979 CADP was to establish a panel for the purpose of hearing the dispute.[33]

When the 1979 CADP acted as a dispute settlement body, it was to operate as a lower-level tribunal so that parties dissatisfied with its recommendations had the right of 'appeal' to the GATT panels. Under the GATT, contracting parties reserved the right to supervise the operation of the General Agreement.[34] In addition, dispute settlement by the 1979 CADP was to be governed, *mutatis mutandis,* by the provisions of the Understanding Regarding Notification, Conciliation, Dispute Settlement and Surveillance.[35] In 1980, the 1979 CADP decided that the measures it was empowered to authorize could include those authorized under Articles XXII and XXIII of the GATT.[36] In effect, the 1979 CADP was now to be an important element in the resolution of antidumping disputes. Through it, signatories to the Code began the preliminary moves towards the resolution of complaints.

Granting powers of dispute resolution to the 1979 CADP, it is argued, was a consequence not only of the lack of time for the negotiators to harmonize the provisions on dispute settlement in the various agreements and bring them into line with those of the GATT[37] but also of the specific nature of each subject.[38] Either of the two following hypotheses can probably explain why a dispute settlement role was assigned to the 1979 CADP.

First, the DCs were the contracting parties least likely to utilize the GATT dispute settlement procedures.[39] A general mistrust of the dispute settlement process and apprehension about the costs of a dispute made the DCs wary of international trade legalism, even though it was generally in their interests. Between 1947 and 1979 the DCs filed no antidumping complaints before the panels. This avoidance of antidumping complaints applied to the period when they increased their rate of filing petitions on GATT issues in general. Arguably, then, although the 1979 CADP might have been of value as a forum to discuss antidumping issues, the DCs would not be inclined to use it as a tribunal for the resolution of antidumping disputes. Given the increase in antidumping measures adopted by the developed countries from the late 1970s,[40] it is possible to construe the judicialization of the 1979 CADP as a strategic move by the advanced countries to exclude the DCs from full participation in the 1979 CADP.

Second, as noted above, the DCs had started to express concern about the calculation of their home-market prices by antidumping authorities in the developed countries. Arguably, developed-country signatories to the 1979 Code realized that the DCs might increase their interest in the workings of the 1979 CADP and, ultimately, become signatories to the 1979 Antidumping Agreement. The result of this would most probably be a sharp change in the tenor of discussion in the 1979 CADP, with it now reflecting North–South tensions over international trade. As a consequence, consensus on antidumping might become hard to reach. In effect, the stable relationship among the developed countries in the 1967 CADP would probably come to an end. Linked to this was the probability of complaints filed before it alleging violation of DC rights under the Code. Therefore, empowering the 1979 CADP to hear disputes was most probably a result of anticipated friction in the GATT system.

Not only was the design of the 1979 CADP shaped by DCs but they also had an impact on its practice. In 1980 the 1979 CADP adopted a decision that had significant implications for DC participation in its deliberations. This decision was based on Article 13 of the 1979 Antidumping Code, under which the developed countries were to take into account the special situation of the DCs when they considered the application of antidumping measures. The decision noted that DC export prices could vary from their domestic prices without there necessarily being a finding of injurious dumping.

The significance of the decision was that such price differentials were not to be construed as an intention on the part of the DCs to dump goods in foreign markets.[41] In view of the infrastructural and administrative problems that the DCs faced, the decision also empowered the 1979 CADP to waive obligations relating to deadlines and investigation procedures that would have been binding on any DC that signed up to the 1979 Antidumping Code.[42]

The decision on the special situation of DC economies was a volte-face by the developed-country contracting parties from their position in 1978. Why was there this change in attitude and policy in the 1979 CADP? The usual explanation would probably be that the developed countries' decision was influenced by the notion of Special and Differential Treatment for DC contracting parties to the GATT.[43]

However, given that the DCs had been granted observer status in the 1979 CADP, they were now perhaps more aware of how developed countries abused antidumping laws. In effect, recognition of the DCs' special circumstances was most probably a compromise whereby the signatories could continue to manipulate the antidumping system provided the DCs were given some consideration whenever they were the targets of an antidumping investigation in the developed countries.[44]

Another interesting characteristic of the relationship between the DCs and the 1979 CADP is illustrated by the latter's dispute resolution powers. When it played a role in dispute settlement, one would have assumed that the DCs, especially the NICs, would use it regularly as a tribunal to protect their rights under the 1979 Code. This was because in the 1980s there was a surge of antidumping investigations against DC, particularly NIC, exports.[45] However, the evidence points to the opposite. Only rarely did the 1979 CADP play a role, namely in *United States – Antidumping Duties on Gray Portland Cement Clinker Imported from Mexico*[46] in 1991 and in *EC – Imposition of Anti-Dumping Duties on Imports of Cotton Yarn from Brazil*[47] in 1994.[48]

What is even more puzzling is that this was in the face of the DCs losing most antidumping actions initiated by developed countries at the national level. With regard to antidumping cases in the EC, data for the period 1980–90 indicate that DCs as a whole faced a total of 238 antidumping actions. Of these only 65 petitions were rejected; 101 resulted in the imposition of antidumping duties and 72 were settled through price undertakings. With specific regard to the NICs, they were investigated 71 times. Of these, 21 cases were rejected, 34 cases resulted in antidumping duties and 16 cases were settled through price undertakings.[49]

This pattern was pronounced in Canada, where between 1980 and 1989 DCs were the subject of 73 unfair trade investigations.[50] Of these, 29 were antidumping investigations initiated against the NICs, with 'effective price increases' (the imposition of an antidumping duty on investigated goods or acceptance of price undertakings[51]) existing in 22 cases.[52] Of course, not all DCs which had adverse findings made against them were signatories to the 1979 Antidumping Code.[53] However, as the NICs were the main targets of antidumping actions by the developed countries, it is most probable that this class of DCs would have been more likely to rely on the 1979 CADP to resolve disputes.

The failure of the DCs to use the 1979 CADP was further complicated by a revival in the use of the GATT dispute settlement machinery[54] and by the likelihood that the DCs were beginning to have some faith in the GATT dispute settlement system.[55] How then can we explain this non-use of the 1979 CADP by the DCs to resolve antidumping disputes? One probable reason is that they had very little knowledge of antidumping issues.[56] DCs have complained that antidumping laws are very complex and difficult to understand, as well as costly to implement. DCs claim that the advanced countries have exploited this complexity and cost factors to monopolize the initiation of antidumping investigations. The advanced countries' repeated use of antidumping laws has given them a 'learning' advantage over the DCs in the implementation of antidumping laws, the initiation of antidumping investigations, and arguing antidumping complaints before GATT panels. Hence the DCs have tended to avoid using the GATT antidumping system.

A second probable explanation is that the supposed faith of the DCs in the GATT dispute settlement system was exaggerated and thus they were probably still apprehensive about submitting complaints. This was because, notwithstanding special procedures instituted to protect their interests,[57] even if a case were won compliance with the determinations of the GATT panels would probably still not be forthcoming.[58] This was compounded by a fear of reprisals by the developed countries if the DCs challenged a developed country's antidumping action before the 1979 CADP.[59]

However, other reasons might explain DC behaviour in the CADP. First, although antidumping investigations and duties do serve to stifle international trade, the economically advanced DCs (the NICs) were actually expanding their share of world trade during the period when they were at the receiving end of an increasing number of antidumping actions. For instance, South Korea's exports grew in real terms by 18 per cent per annum after 1970. In most years this rate of growth was above 20 per cent, and in five years during this period it was above 50 per cent.[60]

Nor is there evidence to suggest that Taiwan's exports declined as a consequence of developed-country antidumping actions. On the contrary, research points to an increase. For example, electronic products, which made up barely one per cent of its export, accounted for 18 per cent by the early 1980s.[61] The same can be said for Hong Kong. As a case in point, exports of watches and clocks expanded by 56 per cent per year from the 1960s to the 1980s.[62] Exports of miscellaneous plastic goods also grew on average by 37 per cent per year over the same period.[63] Singapore's economy was just as dynamic: exports grew by 234 per cent between the 1960s and the early 1980s.[64]

By the latter part of the 1980s, when, as noted above, the use of antidumping actions against the NICs reached its peak, the increased growth in exports from the NICs had hardly abated. For instance, between 1981 and 1986 Singapore recorded a steady increase in the volume of its exports; only in 1984–5 was there a marked fall.[65] Exports from Hong Kong also rose dramatically in this period. In 1980, Hong Kong's exports were valued at $19.2 billion, and it was ranked seventeenth among the leading world exporters. By 1988 the value of its exports had risen to $63.17 billion, and it had become the tenth largest exporter.[66]

South Korea and Taiwan exhibited a similar pattern of growth and development in the 1980s. South Korea's trade dependency, particularly its export dependency, had risen from 2.4 per cent in the 1960s to 11.6 per cent in the 1970s. It was well over 30 per cent in the 1980s. By 1991, electronic goods were its largest export sector (28 per cent); textiles were on the decline and raw materials had virtually disappeared from its top exports.[67] Taiwan's exports grew from $5.3 billion in 1975 to $30.4 billion in 1984.[68]

This argument is not intended to diminish the impact of antidumping actions on world trade. Neither is its purpose to question the fact that in the period under discussion the NICs bore the brunt of developed-country antidumping actions. Perhaps in the absence of antidumping investigations in the advanced countries, the NICs would have captured an even larger share of their lucrative markets. But the point made here is that the NICs were able to withstand the impact of protectionism in developed-country markets and thus that this lessened their need for multilateral mechanisms for dispute resolution, i.e. the 1979 CADP. Therefore, the 1979 CADP as a tribunal was largely irrelevant for the key targets of developed-country antidumping investigations. In effect, although the assumption of a dispute settlement role by the 1979 CADP can be partly explained by potential North–South confrontation over antidumping issues, this confrontation never emerged, largely because the main target countries still enhanced their exports despite developed-country protectionism.

What about the results of national antidumping determinations from the end of the Tokyo Round? Can we also explain the failure of DCs to use the

1979 CADP as a dispute resolution mechanism by the fact that tribunals in the developed countries were a more effective and reliable forum? Compliance with international law has always been a problem. State sovereignty serves to create uncertainty with regard to securing compliance with the decisions of international tribunals. However, this is not the position at the national level. The rule of law, a marked characteristic of dispute resolution in the developed countries which target DC goods with antidumping actions, ensures compliance with national judicial determinations.

But for all the effectiveness of national judicial systems, the facts indicate that there was still a real likelihood of an unfavourable outcome to an anti-dumping action initiated against DC imports by the main users of antidumping investigations. One antidumping scholar has noted that 75 per cent of cases involving DCs as respondents were concluded with an 'affirmative final determination'.[69] What this implies is that even if national judicial systems were safe insofar as compliance was concerned, there was still the strong probability that the DCs would lose antidumping cases at this level.

What then does explain the failure to use the 1979 CADP to settle antidumping disputes? Arguably, the attraction of voluntary export restraints (VERs) is one answer. Some of the final determinations against the DCs, 15 per cent to be precise, were negotiated VERs.[70] Although they supposedly have a negative impact on the industry in the exporting country, the point has been made that VERs are still preferred to antidumping duties.[71]

First, VERs were illegal under the GATT.[72] Therefore, exporters could persuade authorities in importing countries to adjust the VER to suit their needs. Also administering and monitoring VERs tends to be quite difficult. There is a variety of ways to circumvent the discipline of VERs, including transhipment of the product in question, upgrading the goods, or exporting them in a less processed form.[73]

Added to this is the issue of quota rents accruing to exporters under VERs whereby exporters, given the forced reduction in the volume of exports, stand to gain from the rise in prices that this artificial decline in output creates.[74] We can assume here that accepting VERs was probably one reason that made filing petitions with the 1979 CADP unnecessary.

Another probable explanation for the non-use of the 1979 CADP by the DCs is that some antidumping actions were settled through agreement on price undertakings. Price undertakings are agreements between importer and exporter to accept revised prices of exported goods in place of anti-dumping duties.[75] Price undertakings are also supposed to reduce international tensions that an antidumping investigation may cause.[76] In effect, investigating authorities prefer price undertakings to antidumping duties.

Moreover, there is the view that price undertakings are to the advantage of the exporting firm. Foreign firms that are the targets of antidumping investigations may want to settle an antidumping investigation by accepting an undertaking if they conclude that they too can gain from an agreement. Indeed, even in instances when it is unlikely that an affirmative determination will be made, resulting in no antidumping duties, exporters may still opt for price undertakings as this might allow them to raise the prices of their exports. The domestic firms that petition their national authorities for relief through antidumping duties may also choose to settle because pursuing the complaint might not now be in their interest. Thus, price undertakings can promote collusion that is beneficial to the parties involved; and this makes them acceptable alternatives to antidumping actions and duties, as both sides can earn greater profits.[77]

In this context, we should note that the EC preferred to terminate antidumping investigations through the use of undertakings when dealing with DCs in general (although this was not always the case when it investigated only the NICs).[78] Australia, one of the main users of antidumping actions, also relied on price undertakings to settle investigations in two out of the five cases that involved DCs.[79] Although the United States was not too enthusiastic about price undertakings at the time,[80] even after a positive determination had been made, its investigating authorities tended not to collect antidumping duties[81] and thus did not really harm firms that were the targets of antidumping investigations. As a consequence of the above considerations, the 1979 CADP was not of much importance to the DCs as a dispute resolution body.

GATT TEXTILES AND CLOTHING COMMITTEES

Since the inception of the GATT, DC views have tended to differ from the views of the developed countries on how it should regulate trade in textiles and clothing. Whereas the developed countries wanted to maintain state intervention and the imposition of quotas, the DCs were seemingly in favour of the application of free-market principles. As a consequence of this, a series of arrangements have existed since the late 1950s to regulate international trade in textiles and clothing.

The first was the Short-Term Arrangement on Cotton Textiles (STA) of 1959.[82] The parties to the STA agreed to establish the Provisional Cotton Textiles Committee (PCTC).[83] The PCTC was charged with working towards a long-term solution to the problems arising from the international trade in textiles, collecting data for this purpose and making recommendations for a long-term solution to those problems.[84] Compared with later institutional structures for the supervision of trade in textiles and clothing, this was a limited mandate. However, the PCTC functioned for only one year, and was replaced by the Cotton Textiles Committee (CTC), established under the Long-Term Arrangement on Cotton Textiles (LTA).[85]

The CTC had a wider range of functions than its predecessor. It was authorized to undertake studies on trade in cotton textiles as the participating countries decided,[86] to collect statistical and other information necessary for the discharge of its functions,[87] to discuss divergences of views on the interpretation of the LTA,[88] to review the operation of the LTA[89] and to decide whether to extend, modify or discontinue it.[90]

The CTC was created when the contracting parties acknowledged the development of a new situation: 'market disruption', defined as a sudden substantial flow of very low-priced imports, often from a small number of exporters.[91] Thus, on the face of it, the CTC's concept of market disruption limited DC textile exports. However, the DCs did try to exploit the CTC in order to achieve their trade objectives. For instance, they tried to get it to clarify the definition of 'market disruption' by recommending that the meaning of the word 'substantial' should be more precise.

Despite its expanded competence (compared to the PCTC), the CTC was a weak institution, and was generally regarded as one of the reasons for the LTA's failure.[92] To some extent, the CTC's flaws can be explained by the DCs' impact on the world textiles trade. First, there were underlying tensions between exporters and importers as to how that trade should be regulated. A consequence of this was that in its early years the CTC failed to respond meaningfully to DC demands. For instance, in spite of the decision on market disruption, the CTC did not have the power to decide on whether disruption had taken place. Instead, it merely stated that there should be periodic bilateral exchanges of views between the parties on this matter.[93]

Moreover, the LTA did not give the CTC substantial powers to resolve disputes. Although its recommendations were to be taken into account if a complaint it heard were subsequently brought before the GATT panels under Article XXIII of the GATT,[94] it only had recommendatory powers in two instances: when there were differences over the interpretation of the LTA[95] and when there was an allegation that a participating country's interests were being seriously affected by measures adopted by another participating country.[96]

On the face of things, it would seem that circumscribing the role of the CTC was detrimental to DC interests. This is because, arguably, a strong CTC might have been able to help prise open developed-country textile markets, ostensibly the DCs' ultimate aim. However, it can be contended that some DCs either deliberately helped to design a weak CTC or tactically acquiesced in the shaping of this institution's powers. This was because not all the DCs were against securing greater market access through bilateral negotiations.[97] A multilateral approach, with the CTC as a supranational institution, was most probably a potential threat to their interests. In addition, although the LTA was protectionist, DC exports of textiles increased twentyfold between 1967 and 1973.[98] This volume might have been exceeded if the LTA had not existed, but it is still probable that in view of this increase in exports, a strong CTC was not really needed at this time.

THE MULTIFIBRE ARRANGEMENT AND THE TSB

The Multifibre Arrangement (MFA)[99] was adopted in response to the flaws of the LTA. The first MFA was concluded in 1973. It continued in existence, through an extension agreement, until 1994.[100] The MFA permitted trade restrictions either through bilaterally agreed quantitative restrictions or through unilaterally imposed restraints.[101] Its importance for the DCs derived from the fact that textiles and clothing accounted for about 45 per cent of the OECD states' imports from DCs. Given its general restrictive effect, its impact on trade was substantial.[102]

One rationale put forward for the LTA's failure was the lack of a strong supervisory body to monitor trade restrictions imposed by the participants and, where necessary, to resolve disputes.[103] Acknowledging the weakness of the CTC, the MFA provided for the Textiles Surveillance Body (TSB).[104] The TSB was created to supervise the MFA and settle any disputes that might emerge.[105] The DCs were critical of the TSB's composition. They argued that its framework was skewed towards the developed countries. They alleged that by allocating three of its eight seats to the US, the EC and Japan, the TSB made certain of developed-country continuity in its work. This, however, was an advantage denied to the DCs, as their representatives were never permanent.[106] Participation in TSB sessions for shorter times than those of the advanced countries' representatives would limit DC representatives' ability to learn more about the operation of the MFA and to gain a greater understanding of how the MFA and the TSB could work to their advantage.

From the DC's point of view the TSB was further weakened by the EC's interpretation of its role. The EC insisted that the TSB was an organ of conciliation, as distinct from an arbitral and judicial body.[107] The significance of this position was appreciated by the DCs when they acknowledged the EC's role and power and that it was virtually impossible to guarantee the MFA's success without EC cooperation.[108]

Apart from their views on the unsatisfactory nature of the TSB, there was no unity among the DCs, within the TSB, as they failed to adopt unified positions on key issues.[109] DCs' positions on the nature of the MFA were influenced by how their national decision-makers perceived the competitive position of their textile industries. As a result of their different perceptions, three groups emerged from within the DCs. The first group was made up of highly competitive textile exporters (Hong Kong, South Korea, Taiwan and Singapore). It argued for the international textile trade to be determined by market forces. This was because its members knew they would penetrate the markets of developed countries relatively easily. This group preferred a strong TSB, as it believed in multilateral initiatives to overcome developed-country protectionism.

The members of the second group (India, Brazil and Pakistan) were competitive in some products owing to their comparative advantage and were competitive in other products because of MFA restrictions placed on the first group of countries. Thus the position of this group was less clear than the first group's. With regard to products in which its members were highly competitive (such as cotton-based products), they wanted the international trade in textiles to be guided by market forces. But their position did not apply to international trade in products in which they were not competitive. Here they were in favour of selective controls.[110] Thus, as far as the TSB was concerned, their attitude varied. They preferred a strong TSB only when trade in their weak products was under consideration.

The third group (Thailand, Sri Lanka and Latin American countries other than Brazil) had either uncompetitive textile industries or a very small share of the world market. Its members could benefit by exploiting MFA restrictions on the more competitive countries.[111] This group was not wholly against bilateral textile agreements in principle, and it did not mind if the TSB were a strong institution, as multilateralism could be a barrier to its attempts to reach favourable bilateral arrangements.

However, establishing the TSB did have some advantages for the DCs. As a supervisory institution, it could help them to improve their weak bargaining position in bilateral dealings with developed countries.[112] Also, although its recommendations were non-binding, Article 11 (8) of the MFA gave it some authority by stating that participating countries shall endeavour to accept in full the TSB's recommendations.[113] In addition, the small size of the TSB (compared to the PCTC) was conducive to arriving at a consensus. It was now relatively easier for it to resolve disputes and to help prevent new ones from emerging.[114]

As was the case with the 1979 CADP, the DCs hardly ever used the TSB to resolve disputes. There were two reasons for this. First, the trade in textiles was excluded from the tight discipline of the GATT. Hence, the DCs could not be guaranteed whatever protection was afforded by the GATT dispute settlement procedures.[115] This was the outcome of *Norway – Restrictions on Imports of Certain Textile Products*, when Norway refused to implement the panel report that had upheld Hong Kong's challenge to its cutbacks in textile quotas.[116]

Second, although the MFA was protectionist, there was still a rise in the volume of imports from the DCs in the 1980s. US imports of textiles rose so rapidly from 1981 to 1986 that critics suggested that this was a result of MFA III's ineffectiveness.[117] Between 1982 to 1986, the real volume of American imports of textiles and apparel rose by 94 per cent and 105 per cent respectively.[118] It was not only the United States that saw a rise in the volume of DC imports; there was also a spurt in cheap imports into the EC of around 6.5 per cent per year.[119] In addition, restraints imposed by importing countries created an artificial scarcity of textiles and apparel. This drove up their price and created windfall gains which were shared, *inter alia*, among exporters.[120] In sum, although the design and functioning of the TSB was, ostensibly, important to the DC signatories to the MFA, in practice their textile exports still increased even without a strong multilateral institution.

GATT AGRICULTURAL COMMITTEES

Although there was no agreement on agriculture in the early years of the GATT,[121] the contracting parties did try to redress problems of the world trade in agriculture. One measure in this direction was the Programme of Action Directed Towards an Expansion of International Trade.[122]

The contracting parties established three committees for this purpose. Committees I and III were to examine the possibility of a further round of multilateral tariff negotiations and other measures, and of the expansion of trade (particularly the maintenance and expansion of DC export earnings), respectively. Committee II was charged with gathering data on non-tariff barriers to agricultural trade as well as data on income support for agricultural producers; examining the effects of non-tariff and income-support measures on trade in agricultural products; considering how the rules of the GATT had proved inadequate to promote the expansion of international trade in agricultural products; reporting on steps that might be taken in such circumstances; and suggesting procedures for further consultations between all contracting parties on agricultural policies as they affected international trade.[123]

Was this first committee on agriculture (CAG) designed to serve DC interests? It would seem that its framework suited the DCs. First, the WTO CAG was under an obligation to consult with the United Nations Food and Agricultural Organization (FAO). This provision favoured the DCs.[124] The FAO is committed to enhancing food security for DCs. This includes bettering the conditions of rural peoples and the expansion of the world economy. Thus it was a success for them to secure a role in assembling data that was key to exposing protectionism in their export markets.

Second, the CAG decided to use consultations among the contracting parties as a means of enhancing transparency in world agricultural trade. In its view, consultations would provide an appropriate and valuable means of understanding how global agricultural markets worked. They would also serve as one of the bases for its further work.[125] The CAG agreed that its consultations should focus on the impact of agricultural policies on international trade so as to improve understanding of its related problems and to expand trade in accordance with the objectives of the General Agreement.[126]

However, the CAG's powers were limited. It did not really achieve much in articulating DC desires for greater access to EC and US agricultural markets. This is not surprising, as there was no agreement on agriculture and thus the CAG had nothing to enforce. In the absence of an agreement, it is doubtful whether the DCs' influence would have counted for much even if they had seriously influenced the CAG.

As was the case with the textiles committees, it is questionable whether the DCs really wanted to see a very powerful CAG. This would probably have attempted to enhance open markets in agricultural products. Although the DCs were enthusiastic about exporting agricultural produce to overseas markets, some of them were guilty of agricultural protectionism in a manner akin to practices in developed countries.[127] As a consequence, a weak CAG, which was reduced to being merely a forum for discussion, was suited to their objectives. Not surprisingly, the records of the CAG do not reveal any DC attempts to reinforce its authority and thus make it an important component of the GATT committee system.

Besides, agricultural exports were no longer a policy priority for some DCs. They saw the export of manufactured goods as key to growth and development. Between 1959–61 (when the first CAG was established) and 1967–9, the share of agricultural exports in the total exports of all DCs fell from 51 per cent to 39 per cent.[128]

There was also the issue of the agricultural lobbies in Europe, the United States and Japan, which were wary of bringing agriculture under the umbrella of the GATT. In the 1960s, they determined to prevent the trade in agricultural products from being subjected to the discipline of the market.[129] For this reason, they resisted attempts to open up world trade in farm produce.

Probably, therefore, the DCs failed to see the need for a strong CAG or could not muster enough support for such an institution. The same could be said concerning the CAG established in 1967.[130] This committee was charged with examining the problems of the agricultural sector and exploring the opportunities to attain the objectives of the General Agreement in the area of agriculture.[131] Like its predecessor, the 1967 CAG was given a mandate to deal with any aspect of world trade that was not integrated into the GATT.[132] It was to make recommendations with a view to achieving greater liberalization in the trade of agricultural products.[133] However, by the launch of the Uruguay Round it had accomplished very little.

The rulings of the GATT panels in cases involving agricultural products were additional evidence of the probability of a strong CAG ruling against DCs in the event of international trade disputes, and this reinforced any DC misgivings about the creation of a strong CAG. Robert Hudec's analysis of agricultural trade cases supports this point.[134] Hudec examined 207 cases by dividing them into agricultural cases and non-agricultural cases. He found that in the first decade of the GATT, 23 per cent of its caseload involved disputes over trade in agricultural produce. By the 1960s, this had risen to 86 per cent of all cases. In the 1970s, the figures had slipped back to 53 per cent, and fell further still in the 1980s, to 47 per cent.[135] Over the 42-year period of Hudec's study, the GATT panels ruled in favour of plaintiffs in 84 per cent of the agriculture cases that they heard. The peak period was the 1980s, when the favourable adjudication rate was up to 90 per cent of all agricultural product cases.[136]

In addition, it was obvious that plaintiffs insisted on pursuing cases involving agricultural products. In 62 per cent of these cases there was what Hudec has described as 'full satisfaction', with the 1980s being the period when this was the highest, at 71 per cent.[137] Furthermore, plaintiffs were least likely to settle or withdraw complaints involving agricultural cases during this 42-year period of analysis. On average, complaints failed to go through the entire dispute settlement procedure in only 9 per cent of cases.[138] Pre-panel settlement or withdrawal was most likely during the 1980s – it happened in 13 per cent of all cases.[139]

On the face of it, agricultural complaints were more likely to be settled in favour of the plaintiff than in cases involving non-agricultural goods. The significance of this was that a highly specialized CAG, likely to be more conversant with protectionist practices in all GATT contracting parties, would have posed a greater threat to the DCs' protection of their agricultural markets. Thus a CAG with dispute settlement powers similar to the 1979 CADP or the TSB was not in the interests of the DCs at the time.

This finding is reinforced by Hudec's observation that over the entire period of his analysis, the EC was the most regular defendant in agricultural cases. He argues that this was because the Common Agricultural Policy (CAP) was a highly protectionist arrangement.[140] The inference here is that the LDCs with protectionist agricultural policies would probably not have been spared if the GATT contracting parties had devoted greater effort to agriculture through the drafting of a code and the subsequent establishment of a committee.

CONCLUDING COMMENTS

What can we conclude with regard to DC participation in GATT/WTO committees at the end of the Tokyo Round? The evidence and analysis above suggest that the DCs were casual and/or shrewd observers (as was the case with the CADP and the CAG), or active participants (as was the case with the textiles committees).

However, our analysis of the DCs' behaviour should not discount the possibility that some of them tended to disregard the committees, largely because they had the Committee on Trade and Development (CTD) as a forum for the articulation of their concerns. The CTD was established as a consequence of the contracting parties adding Part IV to the GATT. Part IV was a response to the concerns of the DCs about their access to the markets of the developed countries. Under Part IV, the contracting parties were authorized to establish any institutional arrangements needed to further the objectives set out in Article XXXVI.[141] The CTD was established for this purpose.[142] In effect, given the role of the CTD and the fact that it was charged with examining ways in which DCs could participate more fruitfully in the GATT system, too much concern with the workings of the other committees was, arguably, unnecessary.

3

The impact of developments after the Tokyo Round

For a year after the conclusion of the Tokyo Round, the various code committees were seen as a success, and contracting parties saw them as vital for the strengthening of the GATT system. This success was largely because the committees established procedures for reviewing whether signatories' national practices were consistent with the provisions of the various codes. However, although the committees did engage in serious analysis and discussion of national practices, some observers judged that there were no real legal accomplishments and that in the run-up to the launch of the Uruguay Round they had not reached much agreement on how to further trade liberalization.[1]

As far as the DCs were concerned, they quickly realized the strategic importance of the code committees and thus they demanded a lower level of code obligations so that they could become signatories. DC pressure paid off. In the 1982 GATT Ministerial Declaration the contracting parties charged each committee with examining measures for facilitating greater DC membership of the codes and the committees. As a consequence of a decision taken during the Tokyo Round, non-signatories were given the right to participate in committee meetings.[2] Despite advanced countries' attempts to make this conditional on DCs having limited access to committee documents, all non-signatories were entitled to see all committee documents.[3]

The DCs adopted a more aggressive attitude towards the world trading system by the end of the 1980s. They were now determined to play a role in shaping the outcomes of the Uruguay Round of trade talks. What caused this change in outlook, and how has it been reflected in the DCs' role in the WTO committees?

It is possible that the United States' changing attitude towards the multilateral trading system in the 1980s, characterized by its insistence on reciprocity to the fullest extent,[4] triggered DC interest in the GATT as a whole and the committees in particular. An open trading system tends to be a consequence of the desire of a global hegemonic power to promote trade liberalization. The hegemonic power bears, *inter alia*, the costs of supporting this international arrangement, and in doing so it allows other participants in the system to avoid the full weight of their responsibilities.[5]

In the absence of a hegemon, trade liberalization tends to rest on countries' willingness to comply with obligations they have entered into, and also to abstain from opportunistic protectionism.[6] In effect, with the United States sceptical of the GATT system in the 1980s and thus no longer willing to act as a hegemonic power, it was now imperative that DCs acknowledge the GATT and the probability that reciprocal demands would be made upon them. Thus it was necessary to take seriously the entire GATT system, including its committees.

Another possible explanation is that in the wake of decolonization the view existed that the Third World countries' persistent underdeveloped state was due largely to the impact of colonial rule and the neo-colonial relationship between them and the rich industrial countries. One manifestation of this relationship was the fact that the DCs mainly produced primary commodities for the industrial countries. This generated hostility to the international economy and reinforced the belief that industrialization was the way forward if the DCs wanted to achieve levels of development equal to those of the Western industrial countries. Import substitution became one of the means to attain this goal.

Import substitution meant rapid industrial development, mainly through the protection of DC domestic industries on infant industry grounds, and it was necessary because export earnings from primary commodities were insufficient to support national economic development programmes.[7] As a result, DC foreign trade regimes were designed to support the drive towards industrial development. Policy measures for protection included import licences or outright prohibition of certain foreign goods and the maintenance of high artificial exchange rates.[8]

However, by the 1980s import substitution was seen as a failure.[9] The overwhelming majority of the DCs had failed to catch up with the advanced countries and it was also obvious that their economies were in crisis. This realization, among other factors, led to a change in outlook on the part of DC policy-makers. If suspicion of the international economy had contributed to their economic plight, then perhaps the opposite might lead to the growth rates of the NICs that the DCs admired. This would entail open markets. Invariably this meant that the DCs had to embrace the GATT system, as it was the source of the design of world trade rules.

Just as the DCs were abandoning their hostility towards the international economic system, there was a sudden transformation, in the 1990s, in the broader world economic and political order. The collapse of communism in the Soviet Union and its east European satellites and its replacement by governments committed to free-market economic reforms virtually ended belief in a centrally planned economy. This had consequences for the world trading system, as it undermined the traditional North–South dialogue on an international economic order. The emphasis now was on trade liberalization, and that was the hallmark of the GATT system.

In addition, the so-called Washington Consensus influenced DC attitudes towards trade liberalization. The Washington Consensus is a term in development policy that originally meant the policy consensus on measures to tackle the crisis in Latin American economies, a consensus that emerged from a 'process of intellectual convergence'.[10] It drew on conservative policy initiatives of the Reagan era and incorporated some of them into what was described as 'the intellectual mainstream'.[11] In its original formulation, it was a range of policy reforms stressing that the solution to the poverty of the developing countries lay in the type of economic policies they pursued irrespective of their natural and human capital.[12] Included in these policies was trade liberalization.[13]

The DCs have come to accept the principles of the Washington Consensus, and thus their views on trade liberalization have changed from suspicion of the global economy to faith in the virtues of strengthened international economic relations. Arguing in support of the Washington Consensus, some policy analysts have stressed the importance of institutions, given that its policy prescriptions did not set out the role institutions can play in transforming distressed Third World economies.[14] Thus, not only do the DCs wish to see more open markets but they have also come to appreciate the role that international institutions play in trade liberalization.

The failure of import substitution and the collapse of the communist system led to two developments: a large number of applications by DCs to join the GATT[15] and the weakening of the DCs' leverage in the United Nations Conference on Trade and Development (UNCTAD) through their alliance with the coalition of centrally planned economies.[16] As countries such as South Korea, Singapore and Brazil became strong competitors in world markets in a broad range of manufacturing industries, DC cooperation and strategies within the GATT from the 1960s and 1970s were increasingly seen as unnecessary.[17] DCs were now going to include their individual self-interest when participating in the WTO, and this affected the nature of their role in the GATT/WTO committee system.

THE RECONFIGURATION OF INTRA-DC RELATIONS WITHIN THE GATT

These developments led to a political realignment by the DCs.[18] For instance, with regard to trade in agriculture, Chile, Colombia, Thailand, Uruguay, Brazil, Fiji, Indonesia, Malaysia and the Philippines were in favour of more open agricultural markets, and so they teamed up with some developed countries to form the Cairns group.[19] Differences in outlook also emerged in Asia, with India opposed to the more export-oriented Bangladesh, Singapore, Sri Lanka and Thailand. The same pattern emerged in Latin America and the Caribbean. Countries such as Brazil and Argentina which traditionally had been hostile to increased participation in the world trading system were now willing to join countries such as Chile and Trinidad and Tobago in embracing the GATT.[20]

Apart from developments in the international political economy, relations among DC representatives at GATT headquarters in Geneva also underwent major changes, and this had implications for their participation in the committees. The norm for more than two decades prior to the 1980s was that an informal group of DC contracting parties operated within the GATT. This group, dominated by Argentina, Brazil, Egypt, India and Yugoslavia[21] (the so-called Big Five) and supported by Chile, Jamaica, Pakistan, Peru and Uruguay, assumed leadership on issues affecting the DCs. Although it was not a formal coalition and did not insist on DC compliance with its positions, it had had some success in articulating the DC positions in the GATT until the end of the Tokyo Round.

The 'Big Five' DCs assumed a leadership role largely because of their political importance, which was determined by the size of their economies and populations.[22] Their leadership role in the Non-Aligned Movement and the G-77 served to cement their status.[23] The GATT convention of reaching agreement by consensus[24] also contributed to their importance. Moreover, the five could dominate the negotiations because of the skills of their negotiators in Geneva and the logical validity and appeal of their positions. The consequence of this was that in Geneva no agreement could be reached unless the Big Five DCs gave their support. This position was reinforced by US acceptance and the accommodation of the GATT Secretariat.[25]

By the beginning of the 1980s, the dominant role of the five major DCs was being resented and challenged by a number of other DCs. For instance, the South Koreans had begun to assert their own importance, based on their larger share in international trade in relation to all other DCs. They insisted that the Big Five take their views into account. The Andean group had also become active and wanted a greater role.[26]

The differences among the DCs were manifested in various perspectives

31

on the future direction of the multilateral trading system. The five contracting parties opposed to the inclusion of services in the new round led the first group. Their opposition had become stronger since 1982 because research tended to show that any existing comparative advantage they had would be wiped out if services came to be negotiated multilaterally. The second group was made up of the enthusiasts for the new issues who had extended their support for reasons of either economic advantage or politics. Its principal members were Colombia, Chile, Jamaica, South Korea and Zaire. The third group consisted of countries which had an open view on the issues and would support the general position of the DCs. As we shall see below, this difference of position has played itself out in the WTO committees.

The G-77 itself has also noted the collapse in its ranks and has identified a number of reasons for this. It is a large and disparate grouping and faces an increasing number of complex and interrelated issues. Most G-77 members are inadequately equipped to deal with these issues, hence the South's unequal relationship in negotiations and in the proceedings of multilateral organizations *vis-à-vis* the North. Also, few, if any, concrete results have come from the G-77's activities, and thus doubts have grown about its value. Many national capitals have come to focus on the Bretton Woods institutions and GATT/WTO, where, it is felt, more tangible and immediate issues and benefits are at stake.

The problem here is that in these organizations each DC has acted largely on its own. No group position has been developed and/or pursued with vigour. Owing to the absence of substantive analysis and synthesis concerning its own needs and perspectives, and the difficulties in reconciling apparent differences among its members, the G-77 has increasingly been marginalized by individual delegations or regional group positions or has been forced into largely ineffective compromise positions that try to accommodate everyone.

Even DC solidarity within the CTD is beginning to unravel. This is a consequence of tensions over the benefits of open markets. For instance, observers have noted recent fundamental disagreements between least developed countries (LDCs) and the Small Island States on the one hand and the DCs on the other. This is because the LDCs and Small Island States feel that they are more vulnerable and demand even more special deals on issues such as subsidies.[27] In effect, given the fragmentation of view in the CTD, and thus the realization that it is no longer the cohesive forum for the articulation of like-minded DC concerns, it is now important for the DCs to press their case for market access in the other committees established under the GATT/WTO Agreements.

The importance of the WTO committees is further reinforced by the potential for the WTO system to unravel, with a swing away from the judicialization of the system through the creation of the panels and the Appellate Body back to the old GATT with its focus on the political resolution of disputes.[28] That the WTO system is under stress goes without saying. The launch of the Doha Round of trade talks has underscored the continuing trade tensions between North and South, South and South and North and North.

One probable consequence of major disagreements over international trade is that the United States will withdraw from the WTO system altogether. Should it do so, the impact on the multilateral trading system in general, and DCs in particular, will be immense, as the protection of the WTO's rules will be lost. We should note that there are already signs in America of an increasingly hostile attitude towards international law and international institutions in general. Its rejection of the UN as the 'sole source of legitimacy'[29] and the view that participating in the international system is an investment for the United States and not an act of charity[30] are fuelling its hostility towards, *inter alia*, the WTO. Although this in itself does not necessarily mean that America will prefer bilateralism or regionalism over the WTO, arguably its continuing commitment to the WTO will depend to some extent on the functioning of the committees. It will depend too on whether trade matters can be settled through discussion in these forums instead of before the panels and/or the Appellate Body, where US influence is tempered by the procedural rules underpinning the WTO dispute settlement system.[31]

Another important development within the WTO that has relevance for the committees is its perceived 'democracy deficit' and the continuing controversy over its legitimacy. Although international trade specialists see the WTO as a crucial institution for the further development of the world trading system, it has come under increasing critical pressure from civil society in recent times. The contention of the anti-WTO lobby is that it is not accountable to anyone. It is not an elected body, and represents the interests of business interests to the disadvantage of the poor, vulnerable and relatively unorganized mass of international society.[32]

The role of legitimacy is that it generates support for an international institution and thus enhances compliance with its mandates and support for its overall objectives. A democracy deficit can lead to the weakening of an institution's legitimacy. The WTO's 'democracy deficit' is manifested as follows. First, decision-making in the WTO receives no direct democratic input;[33] instead, the WTO's policies and authority are determined through various means by its members. This is a reflection of the progressive supranational character of the WTO. The delegation of decision-making powers to supranational organizations raises issues of democratic legitimacy.[34] Although national bureaucrats are subject to legislative and judicial control, this is much more difficult to apply at the supranational level, as, by definition, a supranational body is at the apex of an institutional structure and there is no other institution that can call it to account. Supranationalism thus requires some regulatory mechanism, and the GATT/WTO committees can serve to facilitate one.

Second, there is judicial law-making. Much WTO law-making occurs in the context of dispute resolution. However, WTO panellists, like judges, are isolated from ordinary politics. There are no meaningful legislative checks on the activism of the panels or the Appellate Body or their 'insensitivity' to the impact of their recommendations. The essence of this problem is captured in Sarah Dillon's analysis of the Banana case, the manifestly obvious activism of the WTO panels and the consequences of this for national political constituencies.[35]

The activism of the panels was highlighted in *EC – Regime for the Importation, Sale and Distribution of Bananas*, when the panel accepted the complainants' argument that the violation of the GATT with regard to the import of bananas into the EC could also be construed as a violation of the General Agreement on Trade in Services (GATS). In this dispute, the complainants had argued that the EC regime for the sale and distribution of bananas was inconsistent with the GATS Article II (Most-Favoured-Nation Treatment) and Article XVII (National Treatment) in that it discriminated against distributors of Latin American non-traditional (ACP) bananas in favour of distributors of ACP bananas in the EC.

The panel, in accepting these arguments, concluded that to find the GATS and the GATT mutually exclusive would undermine the value of the members' obligations and commitments to them and hence the purpose and objectives of both.[36] Through its expansive reading of GATT law, therefore, the panel had broadened the interpretation of the obligations under Article I of the GATT to cover a member's obligations under Article II of the GATS, even though there was no evidence that the drafters of these two articles in the two agreements intended them to be read as supporting each other.

4

Developing countries and the WTO committees since the Uruguay Round

The 1979 Antidumping Code was renegotiated during the Uruguay Round and a new agreement was adopted.[1] The WTO Antidumping Code of 1995 amounts to a revision of the 1979 Code through the clarification of hitherto vague provisions and the inclusion of completely new clauses.[2] The Code established a CADP,[3] which differs in its functions from its predecessor. Thus, the 1995 CADP does not play a role in creating panels or in dispute settlement. Is this a consequence of the incorporation of the DCs into the WTO antidumping system?[4] One interpretation of the consolidation of dispute settlement in the DSB is that it enhances efficiency. A single organ responsible for the resolution of disputes has, with very few exceptions, ended forum-shopping, a practice seen as detrimental to dispute settlement.[5]

However, without disputing the validity of this explanation it is possible to argue that the upsurge of DCs as contracting parties in the WTO CADP also accounts for its losing its dispute settlement function. This assertion is linked to the point made earlier that the 1967 CADP was a relatively smaller and more homogeneous committee and thus that there was no pressing need to accord it any dispute resolution powers. Moreover, by the time the 1979 CADP was established, it was increasingly obvious that it would require dispute resolution powers in view of the interest of the DCs.

Also, the DCs saw the 1979 CADP as a forum for expressing their solidarity with one another. This solidarity was probably due to the small number of DC members on the 1979 CADP.[6] DC solidarity is now on the decline, and an increasing number of DC representatives are contributing to the discussions in the WTO CADP without having to rely on a spokesperson. For instance, in one meeting of the WTO CADP, comments on the operation of and perceived problems with antidumping actions came from Egypt, Hong Kong, India, Indonesia, South Korea, Malaysia and Singapore.[7]

In addition, the quality of the DCs' participation relative to their role in the 1979 CADP has improved considerably. This is explained by the fact that DC representatives in Geneva have forged constructive links with their national antidumping authorities. In the past, DC representatives tended to work in isolation, but the practice now is that nationals come from DC capitals to work with their missions on antidumping issues. Building links between CADP representatives and officials from their national capitals is critical for the success of DCs in the CADP. Key staff in home capitals with analytical and policy-making skills provide direct support and guidance to the resident Geneva delegation.[8] Links between trade representatives in Geneva and national investigators have improved information flows and made the DC missions more familiar with their countries' positions.[9]

The creation of the Ad Hoc Group on Implementation of the Committee on Antidumping Practices (the Ad Hoc Committee) has also improved DC participation and influence in the 1995 CADP. The Ad Hoc Committee was established to discuss implementation issues arising from the adoption of the 1995 Antidumping Agreement and to make recommendations to the WTO CADP.[10]

As the use of antidumping investigations by developed-country members of the WTO against DCs has been compounded by the fact that DCs are increasingly subjecting each other to antidumping investigations,[11] increasing clarification of antidumping practices by developed and DC contracting parties is important for DC interests in the global trading system. The Ad Hoc Committee has discussed a range of issues on antidumping, including the period of data collection for a dumping investigation; notification of the government of the exporting member subject to an antidumping investigation; the provision of essential facts under consideration before making a final determination of dumping and injury; and the disclosure of the investigating authority's findings.[12]

At the time of writing, six topics are under review by the Ad Hoc Committee. These are the practical issues and experience of applying Article 2.4.2 of the Antidumping Agreement, the termination of investigations under Article 5.8 in cases of *de minimis* import volumes; the practical issues and experience in cases involving cumulation under Article 3.3; the practical issues and experience with respect to questionnaires and requests for information under Articles 6.1 and 6.1.1, the practical issues and experience of providing opportunities for industrial users and consumer organizations to provide information under Article 6.12; and the practical issues and experience of conducting new shipper reviews under Article 9.5.[13]

The Ad Hoc Committee has also been directed to examine modalities for the application of Article 15, on Special and Differential Treatment, and to draw up recommendations on how to operationalize it.[14] There has been a response to this mandate by the DCs, although it would seem that only the working group on the further clarification of Article 15 interests the larger DCs.[15]

A further development under the WTO CADP of importance to the DCs is the creation of an informal group on anti-circumvention. One of the most contentious issues in antidumping practice has been the circumvention of antidumping duty orders and what, if any, methods should be adopted to deal with it. When the 1967 and the 1979 antidumping codes were negotiated, antidumping regulation was generally thought of as applying to a whole product, produced by a single manufacturer and imported from a specific country. As the growth of multinational corporations and the globalization and rationalization of production have developed in recent decades, however, manufacturers have had a broader range of production options, such as making the components of a product in several countries, with assembly taking place in yet another country.[16]

These increased options have resulted in a series of situations in which producers covered by antidumping orders have avoided them by shifting manufacture of their product to other plants, by having parts shipped to other facilities for minor assembly, by swap agreements or by other methods.[17]

Countries which have felt that circumvention activities did not deserve special penalties generally have expressed concern over the penalizing of legitimate business activities. They have viewed Article VI as having a narrow reach, which requires new dumping and injury findings before duties can be imposed on the 'new' product or country of origin (antidumping orders are product and country-specific), and/or they have focused on the needs and desires of DCs for foreign investment, which arguably could be affected by circumvention duties.[18]

In the Uruguay Round of trade talks, South Korea, Singapore and Hong Kong in particular strenuously opposed anti-circumvention measures, and proposed that the Antidumping Agreement prohibit relief failing a new investigation.[19] As no definitive provisions on this problem in world trade were inserted into the Antidumping Agreement,[20] the DCs have used the WTO CADP to repeat their concerns on anti-circumvention.[21]

For instance, South Korea has used the discussions in the WTO CADP to raise its concerns about US anti-circumvention investigations. The South Korean representative has noted that an anti-circumvention investigation was appropriate only if there were an antidumping order to be circumvented. The justification for continued antidumping measures should be investigated before allegations of circumvention, especially if an application for an interim review of the antidumping measures has been filed before the application for anti-circumvention measures. With regard to this particular issue, the US representative agreed that America would bring the issue to the CADP for discussion should the need arise. Hong Kong, South Korea, Singapore and Indonesia have all also used the CADP to express their concerns about anti-circumvention actions.

The WTO CADP has also raised the issue of technical assistance to the DCs in its deliberations and has secured undertakings by the developed countries to at least report the measures that they have adopted in this regard.[22] Thus the developed countries have reported, for example, their technical assistance activities to the CADP. The United States pointed out that it has assisted on request to members and acceding members. The EU representative has outlined the Union's technical assistance programme, stating that this included seminars for civil servants in countries that were new or future users of antidumping legislation. There were also seminars for managers, exporters and government officials in countries subject to anti-dumping legislation.[23]

In addition, the WTO CADP has scrutinized the role of the WTO Secretariat in providing technical assistance. It has learned that the Secretariat has carried out antidumping workshops, seminars to explain exporters' rights and obligations in antidumping investigations and country-specific programmes, which include detailed technical instructions focused on problematic issues in the administration of trade remedies legislation.[24]

THE TEXTILES MONITORING BODY

The object of the Agreement on Textiles and Clothing (ATC)[25] is to secure the eventual integration of the textiles and clothing sector, where much of the trade is currently subject to bilateral quotas negotiated under the MFA, into the GATT on the basis of strengthened GATT rules and disciplines.[26] Integration is to be in stages, from 1995 to 2005.[27] Although the ATC focuses largely on the phasing-out of MFA restrictions, it recognizes that some members maintain non-MFA restrictions not justified under the GATT. These are also to be brought into conformity with GATT, within one year of the entry into force of the ATC, or they are to be progressively phased out during a period not exceeding the duration of the ATC (i.e. by 2005).

The ATC has a transitional safeguard mechanism that could be applied to products not yet integrated into the GATT at any stage. Under this mechanism the parties are authorized to take action against individual exporting countries if the sanctioning country can demonstrate that imports of a product are entering the country in such increased quantities as to cause serious damage, or threat, to the relevant domestic industry and that there is a sharp and substantial increase of imports from the individual country concerned. Action under the safeguard mechanism can be taken either by mutual agreement following consultations between the parties in question or unilaterally, but any unilateral measures are subject to review by the Textiles Monitoring Body (TMB). Safeguard restraints could remain in place for up to three years without extension or until the product is removed from the scope of the ATC (i.e. it is integrated into the GATT), whichever comes first.[28]

Established under the ATC, the Textiles Monitoring Body is to supervise its implementation.[29] The TMB is a quasi-judicial standing body that consists of a chairman and 10 members. The members are independent and are required to take decisions by consensus.[30] They are required to notify the TMB of all quantitative restrictions they have put in place.[31]

The ATC is due to expire at the end of 2004. However, some parties are sceptical about whether there will be full implementation of the ATC. This is because the great bulk of sensitive integration is left to the very end of the 10-year period. Under the ATC the integration of textiles is to occur in four stages with 49 per cent of products integrated in the final stage, on 1 January 2005. There is a fear that this will cause structural problems for importing countries and that, as a consequence, it may produce political pressures to delay the ATC's full implementation.[32]

Apart from the above threat, protection by the ATC from low-cost foreign competition serves to enhance the future profitability of the textiles sector in the US, thereby inducing investment.[33] Over the years import quotas have helped to make these improvements in the US textile industry possible.[34] In effect, given concerns about the impact of the full integration of textiles into world trade and the obvious benefits of protection to the influential US textiles lobby, we could see a renewal of the ATC in a manner akin to that of the MFA.

What has been the value of the TMB for the DCs? On the one hand, as noted above, a rules-oriented international trading system is a development that is to their advantage.[35] Courts and other tribunals enhance predictability in international trade and also reduce the inclination of governments to rely on their economic and political leverage to resolve disputes, something that the DCs cannot do. In effect, the transformation and strengthening of institutions to govern world trade in textiles from the PCTC of the STA to the TMB is a welcome measure for the DCs. Moreover, the supervisory role of the TMB in determining whether restraints are in conformity with Article 6 of the ATC, its role in monitoring the provisions of the extension of Article 6 safeguards by the sanctioning member,[36] and the fact that it can hear arguments from members affected by its determinations[37] all serve to reinforce its authority as a critical institution for the DCs as they seek to penetrate the advanced countries' textile markets.

Another advantage of the TMB for the DCs is that, on the face of it, the TMB has the power to exercise *de novo* review of determinations made by national authorities regarding restraints under the ATC. The ATC authorizes the TMB to conduct an investigation of the matter, including a determination of serious damage.[38] The language of the ATC suggests that the TMB shall make its own determinations without regard for the parties' factual findings or conclusions concerning serious damage. *De novo* review by the TMB of national authorities' determinations will be crucial to its role as a dispute resolution forum and an efficient institution for promoting the freeing up of the world trade in textiles.[39]

However, in the opinion of some commentators the authority of the TMB to resolve disputes is compromised by the fact that it is possible to appeal against its decisions at the WTO's Dispute Settlement Body.[40] In effect, the TMB is seen only as a lower-level WTO tribunal. Indeed, some DCs have wanted textile disputes to bypass the TMB and be heard in the first instance by the DSB.[41]

How have the DCs related to one another within the TMB? Have they had a cooperative and harmonious relationship or have they filed complaints against one another in addition to complaints against developed-country members of the WTO? Evidence from the work of the TMB indicates that there is an increasing resort to safeguard actions among the DCs. The TMB has made determinations regarding safeguard actions by Colombia against South Korea and Thailand,[42] Turkey against India,[43] Argentina against Brazil,[44] Argentina against Pakistan,[45] and Argentina against South Korea.[46] This is further evidence of the decline in intra-DC solidarity within the WTO committees.

THE WTO COMMITTEE ON AGRICULTURE

The WTO Agreement on Agriculture[47] is aimed at subjecting global trade in agricultural products to market discipline.[48] The rules governing agricultural trade have been crafted to enhance predictability and stability for importing and exporting countries alike, largely through restraints on the ability of contracting parties to intervene in domestic agricultural markets. Governments are now subject to multilateral restraint in the key areas of market access, aggregate measurement of support and export subsidies.[49]

Established in 1995 under the Agreement on Agriculture,[50] the WTO Committee on Agriculture (WTO CAG) has become a forum for the prevention and/or resolution of agricultural disputes. Although it has no express role in dispute settlement,[51] the raising of issues at its meetings is used as informal consultation.[52] In addition, it is used as a mechanism to pressurize members to conform to their obligations.[53] Given concerns by some DCs about the cost of bringing a complaint before the GATT/WTO panels, the WTO CAG serves, and can continue to serve, as a relatively cheap but useful dispute settlement forum.

The WTO CAG also carries out a yearly monitoring exercise.[54] Monitoring the possible impact of the Agreement on Agriculture on the least developed and the net food-importing countries (NFIDCs) is another measure that is in the DCs' interests. This monitoring exercise involves representatives of institutions such as the World Bank, the International Grains Council, the International Monetary Fund (IMF) and the FAO. Representatives of these institutions present statements to the WTO CAG concerning the general impact of the Agreement on some of the DCs.[55]

For example, FAO technical assistance in relation to the Agreement on Agriculture falls into a number of categories. The assistance is mainly in the area of commodity analysis of special agricultural issues of interest to DCs. This analysis includes assessment of the impact of the Agreement on world prices, production, consumption, and the trade of major food commodities and commodities of export interest to DCs. Then there are studies on the impact of world price changes on the food import bills of all the DCs in general and the NFIDCs in particular.

The FAO has also carried out research aimed at identifying export opportunities that may arise for DCs because of changes in the tariff structure of major developed-country markets. In this regard, it has examined changes in tariff escalation and prospects for the diversification of agricultural exports. This research is disseminated and analysed at CAG meetings and thus helps the DCs to understand the complexities of the issues they face with regard to international trade in agriculture.

By way of further collaboration beneficial to the DCs, the FAO made a detailed presentation on developments in the food security situation in the DCs and the NFIDCs at the November 2000 meeting of the WTO CAG. That presentation included analysis of the food consumption and production and the food imports of those countries as well as recent developments in their cereal import bills. An update of this analysis was given to the WTO CAG in June 2001. The WTO CAG has continued to make efforts to advance the rules of implementation regarding food security in NFIDC members.[56]

A consideration that served to discourage DC participation in the WTO CAG in its earlier stages was that it does not distribute food aid, grants, loans or other forms of financial assistance to the DCs. Thus DC trade representatives saw it as being of marginal utility. Instead, they continued to prefer focusing on other multilateral institutions such as the World Bank, the FAO and the IMF.[57] However, there is now much evidence of a growing realization among DCs that the WTO CAG is of considerable strategic importance. Consequently, some DCs have tried to use the WTO CAG to bind the developed countries to Special and Differential Treatment, as set out in the Agreement on Agriculture and as elaborated upon by the WTO CAG. As noted above, the jurisprudence of the GATT/WTO panels is that 'Special and Differential Treatment' is subjective. Realizing this, and determined to enhance fairness in the world trade in agriculture, the DCs have tried to pressurize the WTO CAG to develop rules that would clarify the meaning of 'special and differential' treatment under the Agreement on Agriculture.[58]

For instance, the African group's proposal to the WTO CAG[59] contains submissions on Special and Differential Treatment. The African proposal acknowledges its importance and calls for binding rules about it. The proposal suggests that existing preferences historically accorded to DCs should be binding under the Agreement on Agriculture and that any new or enhanced preferences to be granted to DCs should be made over and above the terms and conditions of existing preferential market access.[60]

In response to such proposals, the WTO CAG has taken account of Special and Differential Treatment of DCs in drafting its notification requirements. It has considered the burden of certain notification obligations, and by establishing notification requirements it has facilitated the implementation and monitoring of the Decision on Least-Developed and Net-Food Importing Developing Countries.[61]

However, and as further evidence of DC fragmentation, not all DCs are keen to uphold the principle of Special and Differential Treatment of their agricultural exports. For example, Uruguay observed in 2001 that although Special and Differential Treatment is important, improved market access opportunities would do more to improve development prospects in DCs. The Uruguay representative noted that some members appeared to believe that a balanced outcome required all agricultural interests of all members to be taken into account, but the best way to do this was to base commitments on each country's comparative advantage.[62]

The representative of the European Communities observed in the WTO CAG that it had become clear that there was no single position for all DCs, just as there was no single position for all developed countries. Japan too saw the problems associated with dividing the members into DCs and advanced countries, as that ignores the diversity of geographical and natural conditions among members.[63]

The representative of Mauritius shared the view of the EC that there was no single developed-country or DC position, and this applied to Special and Differential Treatment. In this representative's view, all countries had legitimate trade and non-trade concerns that had to be attended to; this was demonstrated by the variety of interest groups involved in the negotiations. Mauritius had participated in three submissions, the first with 26 other countries representing a wide variety of positions on non-trade concerns, the second together with eight small island developing states and the third as part of the African group. In addition, Mauritius had submitted a comprehensive proposal in which it highlighted its inherent constraints as a small island DC dependent upon preferential trade agreements.[64]

The South African representative also spoke out on the issue of Special and Differential Treatment, noting that he was encouraged by members' recognition of the special needs of DCs, particularly the need to participate fully in international trade. In the South African representative's view, their needs would have to be met by concrete solutions. The sooner DCs, especially African countries, were allowed to realize their comparative advantages, the sooner they could broaden their export base, address poverty, promote economic growth and development and ensure their integration into the multilateral trading system. This would create larger markets from which all members could benefit.[65] Although DCs had problems peculiar to themselves, Special and Differential Treatment of their exports might not necessarily be the solution.

The WTO CAG is also developing proposals on export credits for agricultural products. During the Uruguay Round, the members resolved under the Agreement on Agriculture to 'work toward the development of internationally agreed disciplines to govern the provision of export credits, export credit guarantees or insurance programmes and, after agreement on such disciplines, to provide export credits, export credit guarantees or insurance programmes only in conformity therewith'.[66]

Developing international disciplines on export credits is important, as the Agreement on Agriculture implies that export credits can be used to circumvent members' export subsidy commitments.[67] DC concerns on the abuse of export credits were articulated in MERCOSUR's proposal to the WTO CAG.[68] MERCOSUR (the Common Market of the South) proposed a definition of 'officially supported export credit'; the identification and listing of the variety of forms of officially supported export credit operations; the identification and listing of types of institutions and programmes to be covered by such disciplines; the terms and conditions for use of such credits; and the requirement for notification of all officially supported export credit transactions that exceed 180 days.[69] Although yet to be adopted at the time of writing, this proposal is indicative of the DCs' determination to contribute to the development of WTO rules on agriculture by using the WTO CAG.

The DCs have also complained in the WTO CAG that their exports still face high tariffs and other barriers in developed countries' markets. In spite of the general consensus in international trade that tariffs are the more transparent form of protection compared to non-tariff barriers and that the tariffication mandated in the Agreement on Agriculture would contribute to market access, the DCs have used the WTO CAG to articulate demands for greater transparency in the administration of tariffs, especially in the developed countries.

The DCs have pointed out that in addition to the generally acknowledged problems of implementating the Agriculture Agreement, namely 'dirty' tariffication and tariff peaks, tariff escalation and unweighted tariff reduction, the developed-country members of the WTO have adopted complex and non-transparent tariffs as a means of frustrating DC market access.[70]

The DCs claim that there has been an increase in the number of tariff lines to accommodate different tariffs applicable to the same product, such as seasonal, in-quota and above-quota tariffs and the more frequent use of non-*ad valorem* tariffs. Non-*ad valorem* tariffs disadvantage DC exporters. They are less transparent and they complicate the comparison of trade restrictiveness across countries and products, creating uncertainties for exporters. In a number of cases, these tariffs also vary according to one or more technical factors, such as sugar content or alcohol content, making them even less transparent.

Non-*ad valorem* tariffs also tend to weigh more heavily against lower-priced imports and are therefore not in the DCs' interests. The use of variable tariffs by the developed countries has contributed as well to creating a non-transparent tariff structure. OECD countries which have bound tariffs at high levels (higher than their non-tariff equivalent) have applied variable tariffs below the binding.

In view of these considerations, the DCs have used the WTO CAG as a forum to suggest the following reforms to tariff structures. Future multilateral trade negotiations should address the elimination of tariff peaks and escalations in developed countries, and an appropriate formula should be used to bring down any extremely high tariffs by large amounts to more reasonable levels. The WTO CAG should also work out a harmonization formula to reduce tariff escalation. Tariff reductions should be weighted, rather than unweighted, in order to ensure that sensitive products in developed countries are not given further protection. In addition, variable tariffs used by developed countries, such as price band schemes, as well as seasonal tariffs should be eliminated. Variable tariffs should only be allowed as a Special and Differential Treatment for DCs.

The overall thrust of the DCs' argument, then, is that tariff structures in developed countries should be made more transparent and less complex. Should the WTO fail to do so, this will hinder DC attempts to develop processing industries and to break into the markets of the developed countries. On the other hand, smaller DCs are apprehensive about import barriers in developed countries falling too fast. They say they depend on a few basic commodities that currently need preferential treatment (such as duty-free trade) in order to preserve the value of their access to richer countries' markets. Rapid tariff reduction is supposedly detrimental to preferential treatment granted them by developed countries. Thus, not all DCs are keen to see the rules governing international trade in agricultural products redesigned, and they have used the WTO CAG as a forum to articulate this.

To tackle problems arising from the nature of tariff structures in developed countries, the DCs should use the WTO CAG to craft agreed methodologies for any future tariffication. This is because the objectives of the Agreement on Agriculture were frustrated by the advanced countries' creative calculations and interpretations of their obligations, and hence exports from DCs failed to penetrate the advanced countries' markets. Such subjective methodologies resulted in the United States, for example, making only a few relatively insignificant changes to its policies in order to comply with its commitments.

The DCs have also focused on the operations of the special safeguards provisions in the Agreement on Agriculture. The special safeguard provisions, emergency restrictions on imports, were designed to protect the WTO members' economies from the destabilizing impact of a sudden surge in imports[71] as a result of the Uruguay Round reforms. They are provisional measures that can be used to tackle not just sudden rises in imports but any consequences of agricultural liberalization. However, unlike normal safeguards, higher safeguard duties can be triggered automatically when import volumes rise above a certain level or if prices fall below a certain level; it is not necessary for a contracting party to demonstrate that serious injury has been caused to its domestic industry.[72] The DCs' concerns in this regard are that their exports should be exempt from special safeguard duties or that only they should be allowed to use special safeguards to protect their domestic industries.[73]

The DCs have actively used the Special Safeguards Mechanism in the Agreement on Agriculture to protect their economies. Recent figures from the WTO indicate that of the 6,072 special safeguards on agricultural products 2,085 have been used by the DCs.[74] Thus if the WTO responds to the above arguments by keeping the special safeguards mechanism or permitting only DCs to use this mechanism in the future, it is very likely that some DCs will continue to protect their economies against imports from advanced countries and other DCs.

The DCs' interests in the progressive reform of the world trade rules governing agriculture have also led them to participate in the process of analysis and information exchange (AIE). The AIE process originated in a recommendation by the WTO CAG, which noted that the negotiations to continue the Article 20 reform process will be conducted in conformity with the timetable and all other provisions contained in that article.[75] Useful experience will be gained by the WTO CAG in reviewing the implementation of existing commitments, and that will enable it to assess whether compliance with these commitments is full and timely. The process of analysis and information exchange will be facilitated and will allow WTO members to better understand the issues involved and to identify their relevant interests before undertaking the mandated negotiations laid down in Article 20.

The DCs have taken advantage of the WTO CAG's analysis and information exchange process. After an early, relatively unenthusiastic stance – they submitted only three papers to the CAG in 1997[76]– the DC's appreciation of the value of the AIE rose; they submitted eight papers in 1998[77] and eight in 1999.[78] By actively engaging in AIE, they evoked a response by the Secretariat to their criticisms. Of the 15 background papers prepared by the Secretariat in relation to the AIE process, five were on matters of specific importance to the DCs.[79]

THE COMMITTEE ON TRADE AND ENVIRONMENT

For the drafters of the GATT, the impact of free trade on the environment was not a major concern.[80] And although the contracting parties established the Group on Environmental Measures and International Trade (GEMIT)[81] in 1971, it did not meet until 1991.[82] GEMIT's mandate was the examination of trade policy aspects of measures to control pollution and to protect the human environment. Notwithstanding its inertia, the DCs were still wary of GEMIT or any similar institution. The essence of their opposition was that GEMIT could be used as an instrument for the green protectionist agenda of the United States and the European Community,[83] and that environmental issues fell outside the WTO's competence.[84] Not surprisingly therefore, this united them against the creation of the Committee on Trade and Environment (CTE), the successor to GEMIT. However, this objective failed, and the CTE was created at the end of the Uruguay Round.[85]

The CTE has a dual mandate. It is to ascertain the relationship between trade measures and environmental measures to promote sustainable development[86] and it is also to recommend to the General Council of the WTO whether any modifications of WTO rules are required and whether those rules are compatible with the 'open, equitable and non-discriminatory nature of the (WTO) system'.[87]

Given the growing concerns over the impact of trade liberalization on the environment,[88] DCs will be faced with two choices: either they rely on deliberations in the CTE to clarify the relationship between an open trading system and the consumption of environmental resources, or they rely on the WTO DSU and, hopefully, vindicate their rights.[89]

Despite their hostility, the DCs have participated quite significantly in the CTE's deliberations. A sample of the minutes of the CTE's discussions reveals a clear picture of how they have participated. For instance, in one CTE meeting[90] contributions to the discussions were made by India, Singapore, South Korea, Nigeria, Egypt, Mexico, Peru, Bangladesh, Pakistan, Hong Kong, Sierra Leone, and Venezuela. Furthermore, a study of submissions made to the CTE indicates that of the total of 60 submissions made by members between 1995 and 2001, the DCs made 30 of them.[91] It is obvious from their role in the CTE that the DCs' participation has been rather robust.

Why have they been so assertive about their rights and interests in this forum? A probable reason is that the Committee on Trade and the Environment is a virtually new institution. In contrast with the case of the CADP, for instance, there have been no previous agreements. Hence the DCs have not had to enter the CTE and instantly confront the more knowledgeable developed countries. In effect, all parties have the same steep learning curve, and thus the DCs are probably not intimidated by the workings of this committee. Some DCs have relied on rather creative processes to make their presence felt in the CTE. The government of Sierra Leone, unable to participate in CTE meetings because of lack of resources, has relied on a London-based professional legal and academic organization to represent it there.[92]

Another development that works to the advantage of the DCs is that the CTE has a pro-trade bias.[93] It is not especially enthusiastic about linking trade to environmental issues, and thus its way of thinking is in line with DC views about the role and direction of the WTO. In addition, the current stance of the WTO panels seems to be against restricting trade in order to conserve environmental resources.[94] In this respect, the institutional inclination within the WTO seems to favour the DCs. However, this does not imply that relationships among the DCs have been devoid of substantial disagreements. In view of the general breakdown of DC solidarity, one author has noted that issues addressed in the CTE could pit any state against another before the WTO panels, irrespective of its level of development.[95]

There is every reason for DCs to choose litigation as the preferred strategy for resolving trade and environment issues. Analysts of the international trading system have continued to argue that litigation is the best approach, for a number of reasons. First, there is the increasing diversity of the WTO members, one consequence of which is that consensus is extremely difficult to achieve.[96] This is compounded by rivalries among the DCs in the CTE.[97] Secondly, for the smaller and weaker parties in the WTO system, in effect the DCs, litigation has a general advantage over discussions in arriving at an agreement on GATT/WTO rules.[98] A rules-based system with dispute settlement mechanisms lessens the tendency for powerful states to impose their will on weaker and smaller states. Thirdly, the results of GATT/WTO environment-related litigation ostensibly favour the DCs' standpoint that concern for the environment is a ploy to frustrate their export drive.

At the time of writing, the GATT/WTO panels have ruled on a number of complaints in which a GATT Article XX defence has been invoked, albeit unsuccessfully. For instance, in *United States – Standards for Reformulated and Conventional Gasoline*,[99] the panel ruled for the plaintiffs, Venezuela and Brazil.[100] However, although on the face of it the ruling in *United States – Import Prohibition of Certain Shrimp and Shrimp Products (Shrimp-Turtle)*[101] seems similar to that in *United States – Standards for Reformulated and Conventional Gasoline*, closer scrutiny of the panel's and Appellate Body's recommendations in the latter case indicates that litigation over Article XX may not be the DCs' preferred approach. Thus a broader reading of the outcome suggests the possibility of the panels accepting the need to balance an open global trading system with protection of the environment.

In *Shrimp-Turtle*, Malaysia, Thailand, India and Pakistan asked for a panel hearing concerning US regulations on the importation of shrimp. The essence of their complaint was that shrimp harvests conducted in a manner inconsistent with the regulations would be subject to a US import ban.[102] The US aim here was to protect sea turtles, supposedly exhaustible natural resources that were being killed because of shrimp-harvesting practices. The panel ruled in favour of the DCs in *Shrimp-Turtle*. It held the US regulation to be an unjustifiable and arbitrary discrimination between the plaintiffs and other contracting parties, and thus the United States could not avail itself of an Article XX defence.[103]

The plaintiffs, however, considered the decision in *Shrimp-Turtle* to be perplexing. For instance, Thailand pointed out that this decision could be interpreted to mean that members are allowed to take unilateral actions on the basis of the manner of production (in this instance, on the way in which shrimp are harvested) and that such measures would be consistent with GATT Article XX provided implementation is not carried out arbitrarily or in a discriminatory manner. This was because in the view of the Appellate Body, the American measures to protect turtles were legitimate environmental objectives under Article XX (g) relating to the conservation of exhaustible natural resources. But what was flawed was the United States' implementation of its measures, because it patently discriminated against the plaintiffs. In effect, the plaintiffs had scored a rather dubious victory, as the Appellate Body indicated that in future it might rule in favour of measures adopted in pursuance of Article XX (g).[104]

This assertion by the Appellate Body is not surprising. It is most probably informed by the preamble to the Marrakesh Agreement Establishing the WTO, which states that:

> Parties recognize that in conducting their trade and economic relations they will allow for the optimal use of the world's resources in accordance with the objective of sustainable development, seeking both to protect and preserve the environment and to enhance the means for doing so in a manner consistent with their respective needs and concerns at different levels of economic development.[105]

The objective of environmental protection and sustainable development promotion has been further elaborated throughout the WTO agreements, for instance, in the Agreement on Agriculture and the Agreement on the Application of Sanitary and Phytosanitary Measures (the SPS Agreement).[106] In the Agreement on Agriculture, members took note of the need to protect the environment and of how it should be taken into consideration when commitments under the reform programme are made.[107] In addition, the preamble of the SPS Agreement reaffirms that no one should be prevented from adopting or enforcing measures necessary to protect human, animal or plant life or health.[108]

Moreover, if DCs want to avoid using the CTE to clarify WTO rules on trade and the environment and thus rely on litigation for this purpose, then they will have to face the possibility that the Appellate Body may shift further towards 'environmentally friendly' outcomes. Further, they will probably have to brace themselves to deal with the complexities of implementing panel or Appellate Body reports and with their consequences for compliance and full vindication of DC rights.

The conclusion of the implementation panel on the *Shrimp-Turtle* decision was that the United States was under an obligation to make 'serious good faith efforts' to negotiate an international agreement on sea turtle conservation. The implementation panel actually acknowledged that there was a standard for this purpose: the Inter-American Convention for the Protection and Conservation of Sea Turtles. Importantly, the panel looked at the way the measure had been implemented following the recommendations of the Appellate Body.[109]

The implementation panel thus did not challenge the United States' assertion of a close link between the protection of sea turtles and the import ban under its national legislation. What it did acknowledge was that the Appellate Body had 'set a line of equilibrium' between the market access that the members of the WTO expected when they acceded to the WTO Agreement and the United States' right under Article XX (g) to adopt legislation designed to conserve an exhaustible natural resource. The implementation panel noted that the Appellate Body favoured a multilateral solution to the problem rather than a unilateral one. The United States was therefore under an obligation to negotiate, but not necessarily to reach an international agreement on, sea turtle conservation.

The ruling of the implementation panel was that the United States had, in good faith and through its revision of the regulations in question, addressed the concerns of the Appellate Body. The implementation panel thus called upon the US and Malaysia to cooperate and agree upon a plan of action for sea turtle conservation that would be acceptable to all interests. Dissatisfied with this ruling, the Malaysians appealed to the Appellate Body, which, however, upheld the findings of the implementation panel.[110]

The environmental jurisprudence of the WTO panels and the Appellate Body[111] serves as a signal to DCs that the WTO might be shifting, ever so subtly, towards a more liberal interpretation of GATT Article XX. Thus, the DCs might be advised to exhaust all possible efforts within the CTE to minimize if not avoid the use of the panels to resolve Article XX disputes in future.

Then there is the related issue of implementation of panel reports. As we have seen, the process of implementation can be convoluted and prolonged. This can only strengthen the hand of interests which believe that measures taken to preserve the environment should take precedence over the WTO's rules. Implementation can thus serve as a means of frustrating speedy compliance and thereby serve as a further barrier to DC exports.

The above argument on the possible future direction that the panels and the Appellate Body might take in environmentally related disputes does not, of course, mean that the CTE is of no long-term significance for DCs. To date, it has managed to fulfil the first part of its mandate – identifying the relationship between trade measures and environmental measures.[112] Some suggestions have been made that the CTE's work be shifted to other WTO committees.[113] This would most probably entail discussing environmental issues in committees such as the SPS Committee[114] and the WTO CAG.[115]

Whether such a development is ideal for the DCs is moot. As the DCs are unable to attend all WTO committee meetings, the dissolution of the CTE would lighten the burden on their representatives. However, the CTE enables the development of specialized knowledge. The DCs' enthusiasm to submit proposals, participate in discussions and prevent the CTE's complete domination by the WTO's larger members indicates that they are happy using the CTE to discuss trade and environment issues.

The CTE has restated that the WTO's mandate does not cover environmental matters *per se*. Rather, its mandate is concerned with trade measures applied pursuant to multilateral environmental agreements (MEAs).[116] Although there has not yet been a GATT/WTO dispute over the use of trade measures applied by a member pursuant to an MEA, some members have reservations about the consistency of certain trade measures applied pursuant to some MEAs. Of particular concern are the discriminatory trade restrictions applied by MEA parties that involve extra-jurisdictional action.

For some WTO members, this creates legal uncertainty; for others, trade measures applied pursuant to an MEA by WTO members should be consistent with WTO rules and disciplines.[117] Clarification of the relationship between the WTO and the MEAs will enhance certainty in international trade and thus reduce any inclination, especially by developed-country members, towards 'green' unilateral non-tariff barriers.

One suggestion is that consultation and cooperation between the secretariats of the WTO and the MEAs should be encouraged, especially during initial negotiations and amendments of MEAs.[118] Cooperation at this level has advantages. It takes discussion and analysis out of the tense, politically charged atmosphere in the CTE and the governing body of a given MEA and places it within the more technical and arguably much calmer secretariats. Political representatives are ultimately accountable to socio-economic constituencies but bureaucrats in the civil service tend to be more insulated from politics.

A relationship between the WTO Secretariat and the secretariats of the MEAs could benefit from a suggestion in the CTE that the WTO Secretariat reinforce transparency, dialogue and cooperation between it and MEAs from the early stages of negotiations to adopt an MEA through to its implementation. This could be in the form of exchange of information, mutual participation in meetings, joint access to documents and databases, and joint briefing sessions, as necessary. A corollary of this proposal is that the CTE/WTO enter into cooperation agreements with competent MEA institutions. These agreements would provide for (i) the WTO Secretariat to respond to requests for factual information about relevant WTO provisions and (ii) MEAs to inform the WTO of all envisaged trade provisions, which would be examined by the CTE. Reports of CTE meetings would be communicated back to the MEA authorities.

While acknowledging the importance of contacts between the WTO Secretariat and the MEA secretariats, some participants in the CTE are of the view that policy dialogue must take place in national capitals, that the WTO and the MEAs must respect their specific areas of competence and that the WTO Secretariat already has the authority to provide factual information about the multilateral trading system.[119]

The CTE, however, has noted that in reality only a limited number of MEAs actually have trade provisions and that there has not yet been any trade dispute over the use of MEA measures. Thus some representatives in the CTE have felt that, in practice, there is no evidence of a conflict between the WTO and the MEAs. In effect, existing WTO rules are sufficient, and so thus the CTE should avoid upsetting this delicate balance. Therefore, any further clarification of the relationship should be *ex post facto* and be made through the WTO dispute settlement mechanism.[120]

Again, the clarification of this relationship can only enhance DC participation in the global trading system. As noted above, the DCs have always been concerned about developed-country attempts to link trade rules with environmental protection. So far, the developed countries have submitted the majority of environmentally related cases to the panels. Thus, if the CTE fails to define properly the relationship between the WTO and the MEAs, DCs will probably face more GATT Article XX disputes.

Some members feel that scope for the use of trade measures applied pursuant to the objectives of the MEAs can be provided, if necessary, through recourse to the existing waiver provisions of Article IX of the WTO. Article IX provides an opportunity for members to seek, in exceptional circumstances, a waiver to a WTO obligation, subject to approval by a minimum of three-quarters of the WTO's membership. A waived obligation is time-limited and must be renewed periodically; and a trade measure applied pursuant to a waiver could still be challenged in WTO dispute settlement forums on the grounds of non-violation, nullification or impairment of rights.

The strictness of Article IX conditions is considered by some to be appropriate for protecting the rights of WTO members in circumstances in which, for example, MEA parties apply WTO-inconsistent discriminatory trade measures against non-parties. This approach, they feel, could provide a measured, case-by-case response to any problems which might arise in the future.[121]

The CTE has also discussed eco-labelling[122] in joint informal sessions with the Committee on Technical Barriers to Trade. Eco-labelling means the use of labels in order to inform consumers that a labelled product is more environmentally friendly than other products in the same category. These labels, granted by a government or privately sponsored agency to (voluntary) applicants from enterprises, are seen as a market-oriented instrument for environmental policy, as they establish no generally binding requirements or bans.

The criteria for the award of these labels call, at least in theory, for an overall assessment of the ecological impact of a product during its life cycle, including production, distribution, use, consumption and disposal. Therefore, eco-labels differ from 'single issue labels', which address only one environmental quality of a product, for instance biodegradability. They also differ from negative labels, which warn that the use of the product may be dangerous.

In markets with consumer preferences for 'green' products, a label is a means of promotion. Moreover, governments and ecological interest groups tend to support eco-labelling schemes, as the promotional effect of a label sets incentives for producers to improve the environmental qualities of their products. And as well as changing the manufacturing design of products in favour of environmentally friendly products and technologies, eco-labelling programmes aim at protecting the environment through raising consumer awareness of the environmental effects of products and thereby changing consumer behaviour.

The DCs see eco-labelling as a non-tariff barrier. Even though existing eco-labelling schemes are voluntary in nature, the view persists that they may distort comparative advantage because of their potential trade-restricting effects. Notwithstanding DC reservations, some representatives in the CTE have argued that if eco-labelling schemes are successful they influence consumer behaviour and that in this respect they can significantly affect market access and conditions of competition.[123] In this context, therefore, the CTE has called for increased transparency in such schemes because transparency can provide accurate and comprehensive information to consumers.

In addition, discussions in the CTE have focused on whether and how the removal of trade restrictions and distortions, in particular high tariffs, tariff escalation, export restrictions, subsidies and non-tariff measures, has the potential to yield benefits for both the multilateral trading system and the environment. Dealing with such barriers to trade is in the interests of the DCs. The CTE has agreed that relevant measures should not apply only to agricultural products. Rather, the removal of trade restrictions should be undertaken with regard to items such as textiles and clothing. Further work on this matter should be undertaken with regard to the benefits that DCs may derive.[24]

5

Conclusions

GENERAL OVERVIEW OF THE STUDY

The introductory chapter noted the three different methodologies used to analyse the role of international law and international institutions: Realism, Institutionalism and Liberalism. It also pointed out how Institutionalists and Liberals have stressed that international law and institutions can shape interstate relations and can, as a consequence, promote cooperative solutions to global problems. International trade relations in particular can benefit from international legal and institutional structures.

It is obvious that law and institutions have structured the interactions within the GATT/WTO system, and to some extent this has benefited the DCs as they confront an increasingly interdependent global economy. Without a strong WTO, without well-functioning committees guided by rules and procedures, the DCs would face the probability of dealing with the unrestrained power of the developed countries. Issues related to trade and the environment and to monitoring the implementation of the Agreement on Agriculture and the Agreement on Antidumping would be shaped by the advanced countries and implemented by them. The benefits to the DCs of an open economy would possibly be lost.

These broad observations overarch the more specific issues discussed in the study. First, the view that DCs are ignorant bystanders in the evolution of the GATT/WTO system needs to be qualified, as evidence does not support it. Rather, clearly defined instances show that their strategy has been tactical participation or non-participation as appropriate.

Second, the DCs have contributed to changing the committees from symbolic forums with very little real impact on the world trading system to institutions that are key pillars in the architecture of the GATT/WTO. This applies particularly to the 1967 and the 1979 CADP and the TSB and the TMB. However, with the compulsory absorption of DCs into the post-Uruguay Round committees, there has been a recent shift in the function of the committees: they have changed from institutions for dispute resolution – a key component of the world trading system – towards arenas for deliberating upon policy. This does not necessarily imply a radical decline in the committees' importance, but it does mean that the DCs have contributed to the subversion of their authority.

It is also clear that the DCs' behaviour in the committees has largely been motivated by economic considerations. This has especially been the case in the relations among them in the post-Tokyo Round era. Although the formative years of the GATT saw solidarity and harmony among the DCs, this began to change from the 1980s. The fragmentation of DC solidarity is explained by a set of factors ranging from economic models of behaviour to the underlying dynamics of group solidarity. Changing economic preferences and the desire to maximize these preferences have reshaped the framework of relationships among the DCs within the committees. Thus, when it was beneficial for DCs to present a united front in the committees, they enthusiastically did so. But, when cooperation became costly in the sense that adhering to the collective DC stance weakened their position, they quickly defected and assumed a much more independent posture.

RECOMMENDATIONS

International secretariats or trading partners to build up DC capabilities are no substitute for an active role by the DCs themselves.[1] Also, as the WTO system develops further and the issues it discusses become more complex, the ability of DCs to participate effectively in committee deliberations will considerably depend on the analytical ability of their governments and of other institutions at home involved in WTO issues.[2] This is particularly so given that the WTO has a rather small secretariat and thus that most analysis of issues and development of positions is done by members, usually in their capitals.[3]

How then can DCs improve their participation in committee meetings? Where possible, DCs which cannot participate in committee meetings should identify and forge links with like-minded DCs which do have representation or the ability to participate. They should develop a formal consultative relationship with them, thereby ensuring that their own interests are reflected in committee deliberations. Another approach, although contrary to the argument that DC solidarity no longer exists as it did in the early years of the GATT, would be for the DCs to determine whether they can pool their resources and representation in Geneva. This could apply to DCs which belong to a particular regional grouping. An alternative method would be to second staff from a poorly represented country to the already established missions of like-minded countries in Geneva.[4]

It is easy for DCs to be wary of an arrangement that will all
countries to represent them in the committees. This is because of p
agent problems that may arise.[5] The central problem here will be how to get
the agent to act in the best interest of the principal when the agent has all the
informational advantages over the principal and also has different interests.
Agency costs are usually a reflection of how difficult it is for the principal to
control the agent and thus ensure he acts in the principal's interest. DCs
would have to devise mechanisms to monitor the behaviour of their agents.
They would also have to avoid a situation in which the traditionally under-
represented and ineffective DC members would not have their views heard.
Failure to do so would recreate the so-called Green Room process among the
DCs.[6]

In practice the problem of principal–agent relationships will be reflected
in the diversity of DC interests and also in the alliances they are likely to
form in view of the WTO's diverse agenda. It is quite possible that the intra-
constituency problems might emerge within these alliances, for example, on
trade in agriculture or antidumping issues.[7]

Owing to disparities in size and power among the members of the WTO,
the notion of their equality is a fiction. In reality, the EU, the United States,
Japan and Canada dominate the WTO. With constraints on their human
and financial resources, the DCs have not been able to make their presence
felt, notwithstanding their growing interest in the multilateral trading system.

This circumstance has led to calls for changes in the WTO decision-
making system. The thrust of the argument has been for the creation of some
kind of executive board similar to the boards of the IMF and the World
Bank. The effect of this would be discussion of issues in the committees by a
small, elite set of decision-makers. This executive arm would be a specialized
body, would have DC representatives and thus would address DC interests
and avoid the current cumbersome system. DCs could thus optimize the
little financial and human capital they have by participating in a much
smaller range of meetings.

However, this is not a realistic option for the WTO because we are
dealing with a contractual setting in which each member has to claim its own
rights and to respond individually in fulfilment of its obligations. Never-
theless, the concept of alliances can still work for the interests of the DCs
and so should be given some thought. It should be noted that to some extent
this has always been the practice within the GATT/WTO system, as
interest groups have developed along either regional or substantive lines.
Thus perhaps the most important strategic issue facing the DCs is whether
to pursue constituency-building on a formal or an informal basis.[8] In the case
of the Caribbean countries, they have the Regional Negotiation Machinery

with its secretariat. It is represented in Geneva (informally because it is not recognized by the WTO) and the member countries pool information and represent one another at meetings.[9]

If the DCs rely on a constituency system, this will allow for swifter decision-making and consensus-formation. Although litigation is the preferred approach in the pursuit of DC rights, the reality is that not all disputes come before the WTO panels. As a matter of fact, it is extremely doubtful whether the WTO panels could handle all violations of the multilateral trading system. Thus, even when committees do not have a formal dispute settlement role, they still have an impact on this aspect of the GATT/WTO system. In such circumstances, therefore, a smaller committee will most probably be relatively quicker in forming a consensus than a committee with all the WTO's members.

It should be noted too that national legislatures are never full all of the time, and it is not rare to have only a small percentage of the members of a national legislature present at a debate. Through this procedure not only will information be shared and scarce human and financial resources used judiciously but DCs will also develop specializations in particular areas and thus improve their overall performance in the committee system.

Forming alliances with non-governmental organizations (NGOs) can further reinforce DC participation in the WTO committees. Admittedly, there is tension between the DCs and the NGOs.[10] The essence of this tension largely concerns the difference in objectives of some NGOs and the DCs. A number of influential NGOs, particularly those in developed countries, are committed to linking trade with social goals such as protecting the environment and promoting labour standards. The DCs contend that these goals are obstacles to their penetration of developed-country markets and that in effect the NGOs are allies in the protectionist struggle waged against them by competing domestic interests in the developed countries.

Thus, the development of links between the committees and domestic constituencies does have its drawbacks. If the Committees develop and deepen links with civil society, and thus serve as a means whereby members of civil society can project their unresolved national social conflicts into the WTO forums, this can easily frustrate the WTO's mandate. In the opinion of some DC representatives in Geneva, issues such as labour standards, the extent of civil society participation, human rights and animal welfare can only distort the efficient working of the WTO system.[11] This is because increasing cooperation with civil society can easily produce a situation in which committee members react to pressure from parochial interests that are hostile to the WTO and its mandate for trade liberalization. Besides, although there is a tendency to see NGOs as publicly motivated actors, evidence has been adduced to the contrary. Research on public interest non-state actors suggests they are motivated by the same narrow attitude that spurs the lobbying activities of private, profit-making firms.[12]

International organizations lack the democratic legitimacy that derives from the electoral process and thus must derive legitimacy from the manner in which they conduct their business. If policies are forged on the basis of widespread international discussion, a process of global consensus-building, then their legitimacy is enhanced. If, by contrast, policies seem to reflect the power of a few large countries, then the legitimacy of the institution is reduced. Legitimacy is reduced as well if the policies seem to reflect special interests.[13] It has been noted above that the emerging supranational structure of the WTO has resulted in challenges to its legitimacy. Thus, in order to 'rewire' it to its members there must be a perceived mechanism of control or a reporting back to national economic and social interests.

The role of communicator is one that the committee representatives can play: they can serve as channels for transparency and feedback, informing domestic interest groups about the direction discussions in the committees are taking and their consequences. Through their interactions at the domestic level, they can also serve as conduits through which ideas from national economic and social interests can filter up into the WTO system in line with the Liberal view of international law and institutions. In this manner, there will always be the feeling that the WTO is not cut off from the people it is supposed to serve.

Appendix

Extracts from GATT/WTO documents

Decision of 5 May 1980 (ADP/2)

1. The Committee, cognizant of the commitment in Article 13 of the Agreement on Implementation of Article VI of the General Agreement on Tariffs and Trade that special regard must be given by developed countries to the special situation of developing countries when considering the application of anti-dumping measures under the Agreement, takes the following decision concerning the application and interpretation of the Agreement in relation to developing countries:

(i) In developing countries, governments play a large role in promoting economic growth and development in accordance with their national priorities, and their economic regimes for the export sector can be different from those relating to their domestic sectors resulting, *inter alia*, in different cost structures. This Agreement is not intended to prevent developing countries from adopting measures in this context, including measures in the export sector, as long as they are used in a manner which is consistent with the provisions of the General Agreement on Tariffs and Trade, as applicable to these countries.

(ii) In the case of imports from a developing country, the fact that the export price may be lower than the comparable price for the like product when destined for domestic consumption in the exporting country does not *per se* justify an investigation or the determination of dumping unless the other factors mentioned in Article 5:1 are also present. Due consideration should be given to all cases where, because special economic conditions affect prices in the home market, these prices do not provide a commercially realistic basis for dumping calculations. In such cases the normal value for the purposes of ascertaining whether the goods are being dumped shall be determined by methods such as a comparison of the export price with the comparable price of the like product when exported to any third country or with the cost of production of the exported goods in the country of origin plus a reasonable amount for administrative, selling and any other costs and for profits.

(iii) It is recognized that developing countries may face special problems initially in adapting their legislation to the requirements of the Code, including administrative and infrastructural problems, in carrying out anti-dumping investigations initiated by them. Accordingly, the Committee on Anti-Dumping Practices may grant, upon specific request and on conditions to be negotiated on a case-by-case basis, time-limited exceptions in whole or in part from obligations which relate to investigations undertaken by a developing country under this Agreement.

(iv) Developed countries Parties to this Agreement shall endeavour to furnish, upon request and on terms to be agreed, technical assistance to developing countries Parties to this Agreement, with regard to the implementation of this Agreement; including training of personnel, and the supplying of information on methods, techniques and other aspects of conducting investigations on dumping practices.

2. The Committee further decides that paragraph 7 of Article 15 of the Agreement is to be interpreted to mean that the measures which may be authorized by the Committee on Anti-Dumping Practices for the purpose of the Agreement may include all such measures as can be authorized under Articles XXII and XXIII of the General Agreement.

COMMITTEE ON ANTI-DUMPING PRACTICES

Decision of 20–22 October 1980
(ADP/M/3)

The Committee, recalling that, in accordance with the Decision taken on 5 May 1980, 'developing countries may face special problems initially in adapting their legislation to the requirements of the Code, including administrative and infrastructural problems, in carrying out anti-dumping investigations initiated by them',

(i) recognizes that Brazil will require a further period of three years to establish an administrative structure and to set up administrative procedures in order to implement its domestic legislation in conformity with the provisions of the Agreement, relating to the imposition of anti-dumping duties, as provided in Article 1;

(ii) notes that Brazil undertakes not to impose anti-dumping duties until such time it notifies the Committee that it is able to proceed with the full implementation of domestic regulations and administrative procedures deriving from obligations of the Agreement which relate to the imposition of anti-dumping duties;

(iii) agrees that this matter will be subject to review after three years from the date of Brazil's acceptance.

1995 ANTI-DUMPING CODE

Article 16
Code Committee on Anti-Dumping Practices

16.1 There is hereby established a Committee on Anti-Dumping Practices (referred to in this Agreement as 'the Committee') composed of representatives from each of the Members. The Committee shall elect its own Chairman and shall meet not less than twice a year and otherwise as envisaged by relevant provisions of this Agreement at the request of any Member. The Committee shall carry out responsibilities as assigned to it under this Agreement or by the Members and it shall afford Members the opportunity of consulting on any matters relating to the operation of the Agreement or the furtherance of its objectives. The WTO Secretariat shall act as the secretariat to the Committee.

16.2 The Committee may set up subsidiary bodies as appropriate.

16.3 In carrying out their functions, the Committee and any subsidiary bodies may consult with and seek information from any source they deem appropriate. However, before the Committee or a subsidiary body seeks such information within the jurisdiction of a Member it shall inform the Member involved. It shall obtain the consent of the Member and any firm to be consulted.

16.4 Members shall report without delay to the Committee all preliminary or final anti-dumping actions taken. Such reports shall be available in the Secretariat for inspection by other Members. Members shall also submit, on a semi-annual basis, reports of any anti-dumping actions taken within the preceding six months. The semi-annual reports shall be submitted on an agreed standard form.

16.5 Each Member shall notify the Committee (a) which of its authorities are competent to initiate and conduct investigations referred to in Article 5 and (b) its domestic procedures governing the initiation and conduct of such investigations.

1979 ANTI-DUMPING CODE

Article 14
Committee on Anti-Dumping Practices

1. There shall be established under this Agreement a Committee on Anti-Dumping Practices (hereinafter referred to as the 'Committee') composed of representatives from each of the Parties. The Committee shall elect its own Chairman and shall meet not less than twice a year and otherwise as envisaged by relevant provisions of this Agreement at the request of any Party. The Committee shall carry out responsibilities as assigned to it under this Agreement or by the Parties and it shall afford Parties the opportunity of consulting on any matters relating to the operation of the Agreement or the furtherance of its objectives. The GATT secretariat shall act as the secretariat to the Committee.

2. The Committee may set up subsidiary bodies as appropriate.

3. In carrying out their functions, the Committee and any subsidiary bodies may consult with and seek information from any source they deem appropriate. However, before the Committee or a subsidiary body seeks such information from a source within the jurisdiction of a Party, it shall inform the Party involved.

It shall obtain the consent of the Party and any firm to be consulted.

4. Parties shall report without delay to this Committee all preliminary or final anti-dumping actions taken. Such reports will be available in the GATT secretariat for inspection by government representatives. The Parties shall also submit, on a semi-annual basis, reports of any anti-dumping actions taken within the preceding six months.

Article 15

1. Each Party shall afford sympathetic consideration to, and shall afford adequate opportunity for consultation regarding representations made by, another Party with respect to any matter affecting the operation of this Agreement.

2. If any Party considers that any benefit accruing to it, directly or indirectly, under this Agreement is being nullified or impaired, or that the achievement of any objective of the Agreement is being impeded, by another Party or Parties, it may, with a view to reaching a mutually satisfactory resolution of the matter, request in writing consultations with the Party or Parties in question. Each Party shall afford sympathetic consideration to any request from another Party for consultation. The Parties concerned shall initiate consultation promptly.

3. If any Party considers that the consultation pursuant to paragraph 2 has failed to achieve a mutually agreed solution and final action has been taken by the administering authorities of the importing country to levy definitive anti-dumping duties or to accept price undertakings, it may refer the matter to the Committee for conciliation. When a provisional measure has a significant impact and the Party considers the measure was taken contrary to the provisions of paragraph 1 of Article 10 of this Agreement, a Party may also refer such matter to the Committee for conciliation. In cases where matters are referred to the Committee for conciliation, the Committee shall meet within thirty days to review the matter, and, through its good offices, shall encourage the Parties involved to develop a mutually acceptable solution.

4. Parties shall make their best efforts to reach a mutually satisfactory solution throughout the period of conciliation.

5. If no mutually agreed solution has been reached after detailed examination by the Committee under paragraph 3 within three months, the Committee shall, at the request of any party to the dispute, establish a panel to examine the matter, based upon:
(a) a written statement of the Party making the request indicating how a benefit accruing to it, directly or indirectly, under this Agreement has been nullified or impaired, or that the achieving of the objectives of the Agreement is being impeded, and
(b) the facts made available in conformity with appropriate domestic procedures to the authorities of the importing country.

6. Confidential information to the panel shall not be revealed without formal authorization from the person or authority providing the information. Where such information is requested from the panel but release of such information by the panel is not authorized, a non-confidential summary of the information, authorized by

the authority or person providing the information, will be provided.

7. Further to paragraphs 1–6 the settlement of disputes shall, *mutatis mutandis*, be governed by the provisions of the Understanding regarding Notification, Consultation, Dispute Settlement and Surveillance. Panel members shall have relevant experience and be selected from Parties not parties to the dispute.

1967 ANTI-DUMPING CODE

Article 17

The Parties to this Agreement shall request the Contracting Parties to establish a Committee on Anti-Dumping Practices composed of representatives of the parties to the Agreement. The Committee shall normally meet once each year for the purpose of affording parties to this Agreement the opportunity of consulting on matters relating to the administration of anti-dumping systems in the participating country or customs territory as it might affect the operation of the Anti-Dumping Code or the furtherance of its objectives. Such consultations shall be without prejudice to Articles XX and XXIII of the General Agreement.

AGREEMENT ON TEXTILES AND CLOTHING

Article 8
Textile Monitoring Body

1. In order to supervise the implementation of this Agreement, to examine all measures taken under this Agreement and their conformity therewith, and to take the actions specifically required of it by this Agreement, the Textiles Monitoring Body (TMB) is hereby established. The TMB shall consist of a Chairman and 10 members. Its membership shall be balanced and broadly representative of the Members and shall provide for rotation of its members at appropriate intervals. The members shall be appointed by Members designated by the Council for Trade in Goods to serve on the TMB, discharging their function on an *ad personam* basis.

2. The TMB shall develop its own working procedures. It is understood, however, that consensus within the TMB does not require the assent or concurrence of members appointed by Members involved in an unresolved issue under review by the TMB.

3. The TMB shall be considered as a standing body and shall meet as necessary to carry out the functions required of it under this Agreement. It shall rely on notifications and information supplied by the Members under the relevant Articles of this Agreement, supplemented by any additional information or necessary details they may submit or it may decide to seek from them. It may also rely on notifications to and reports from other WTO bodies and from such other sources as it may deem appropriate.

4. Members shall afford to each other adequate opportunity for consultations with respect to any matters affecting the operation of this Agreement.

5. In the absence of any mutually agreed solution in the bilateral consultations

provided for in this Agreement, the TMB shall, at the request of either Member, and following a thorough and prompt consideration of the matter, make recommendations to the Members concerned.

6. At the request of any Member, the TMB shall review promptly any particular matter which that Member considers to be detrimental to its interests under this Agreement and where consultations between it and the Member or Members concerned have failed to produce a mutually satisfactory solution. On such matters, the TMB may make such observations as it deems appropriate to the Members concerned and for the purposes of the review provided for in paragraph 11.

7. Before formulating its recommendations or observations, the TMB shall invite participation of such Members as may be directly affected by the matter in question.

8. Whenever the TMB is called upon to make recommendations or findings, it shall do so, preferably within a period of 30 days, unless a different time period is specified in this Agreement. All such recommendations or findings shall be communicated to the Members directly concerned. All such recommendations or findings shall also be communicated to the Council for Trade in Goods for its information.

9. The Members shall endeavour to accept in full the recommendations of the TMB, which shall exercise proper surveillance of the implementation of such recommendations.

10. If a Member considers itself unable to conform with the recommendations of the TMB, it shall provide the TMB with the reasons therefore not later than one month after receipt of such recommendations. Following thorough consideration of the reasons given, the TMB shall issue any further recommendations it considers appropriate forthwith. If after such further recommendations, the matter remains unresolved, either Member may bring the matter before the Dispute Settlement Body and invoke paragraph 2 of Article XXIII of GATT 1994 and the relevant provisions of the Dispute Settlement Understanding.

11. In order to oversee the implementation of this Agreement, the Council for Trade in Goods shall conduct a major review before the end of each stage of the integration process. To assist in this review, the TMB shall, at least five months before the end of each stage, transmit to the Council for Trade in Goods a comprehensive report on the implementation of this Agreement during the stage under review, in particular in matters with regard to the integration process, the application of the transitional safeguard mechanism, and relating to the application of GATT 1994 rules and disciplines as defined in Articles 2, 3, 6 and 7 respectively. The TMB's comprehensive report may include any recommendation as deemed appropriate by the TMB to the Council for Trade in Goods.

12. In the light of its review the Council for Trade in Goods shall, by consensus, take such decisions as it deems appropriate to ensure that the balance of rights and obligations embodied in this Agreement is not being impaired. For the resolution of any disputes that may arise with respect to matters referred to in Article 7, the Dispute Settlement Body may authorize, without prejudice to the final date set out under Article 9, an adjustment to paragraph 14 of Article 2, for the stage subsequent to the review, with respect to any Member found not to be complying with its obligations under this Agreement.

Article 11

1. The Textiles Committee shall establish a Textiles Surveillance Body to supervise the implementation of this Arrangement. It shall consist of a Chairman and eight members to be appointed by the parties to this Arrangement on a basis to be determined by the Textiles Committee so as to ensure its efficient operation. In order to keep its membership balanced and broadly representative of the parties to this Arrangement provision shall be made for rotation of members as appropriate.

2. The Textiles Surveillance Body shall be considered as a standing body and shall meet as necessary to carry out the functions required of it under this Arrangement. It shall rely on information to be supplied by the participating countries, supplemented by any necessary details and clarification it may decide to seek from them or from other sources. Further, it may rely for technical assistance on the services of the GATT secretariat and may also hear technical experts proposed by one or more of its members.

3. The Textiles Surveillance Body shall take the action specifically required of it in articles of this Arrangement.

4. In the absence of any mutually agreed solution in bilateral negotiations or consultations between participating countries provided for in this Arrangement, the Textiles Surveillance Body at the request of either party, and following a thorough and prompt consideration of the matter, shall make recommendations to the parties concerned.

5. The Textiles Surveillance Body shall, at the request of any participating country, review promptly any particular measures or arrangements which that country considers to be detrimental to its interests where consultations between it and the participating countries directly concerned have failed to produce a satisfactory solution. It shall make recommendations as appropriate to the participating country or countries concerned.

6. Before formulating its recommendations on any particular matter referred to it, the Textiles Surveillance Body shall invite participation of such participating countries as may be directly affected by the matter in question.

7. When the Textiles Surveillance Body is called upon to make recommendations or findings it shall do so, except when otherwise provided in this Arrangement, within a period of thirty days whenever practicable. All such recommendations or findings shall be communicated to the Textiles Committee for the information of its members.

8. Participating countries shall endeavour to accept in full the recommendations of the Textiles Surveillance Body. Whenever they consider themselves unable to follow any such recommendations, they shall forthwith inform the Textiles Surveillance Body of the reasons therefore and of the extent, if any, to which they are able to follow the recommendations.

9. If, following recommendations by the Textiles Surveillance Body, problems continue to exist between the parties, these may be brought before the Textiles Committee or before the GATT Council through the normal GATT procedures.

10. Any recommendations and observations of the Textiles Surveillance Body would be taken into account should the matters related to such recommendations and observations subsequently be brought before the Contracting Parties to the GATT, particularly under the procedures of Article XXIII of the GATT.

11. The Textiles Surveillance Body shall, within fifteen months of the coming into force of this Arrangement, and at least annually thereafter, review all restrictions on textile products maintained by participating countries at the commencement of this Arrangement, and submit its findings to the Textiles Committee.

12. The Textiles Surveillance Body shall annually review all restrictions introduced or bilateral agreements entered into by participating countries concerning trade in textile products since the coming into force of this Arrangement, and required to be reported to it under the provisions of this Arrangement, and report annually its findings to the Textiles Committee.

COTTON TEXTILES COMMITTEE

Article 8

The Cotton Textiles Committee, as established by the Contracting Parties at their nineteenth session, shall be composed of representatives of the countries party to this Arrangement and shall fulfil the responsibilities provided for it in this Agreement.

(a) The Committee shall meet from time to time to discharge its functions. It will undertake studies on trade cotton textiles as the participating countries may decide. It will collect the statistical and other information necessary for the discharge of its functions and will be empowered to request the participating countries to furnish such information.

(b) Any case of divergence of view between the participating countries as to the interpretation or application of this Arrangement may be referred to the Committee for discussion.

(c) The Committee shall review the operation of this Arrangement once a year and report to the Contracting Parties. The review during the third year shall be a major review of this Arrangement in the light of its operation in the preceding years.

(d) The Committee shall meet not later than one year before the expiry of this Arrangement, in order to consider whether the Arrangement should be extended, modified or discontinued.

PROVISIONAL COTTON TEXTILES COMMITTEE

Long-term Arrangement

A. Participating countries agree to create a Provisional Cotton Textiles Committee and to request the Contracting Parties to confirm the establishment of the Committee at the nineteenth session.

The Committee shall:

1. Undertake work looking toward a long-term solution to the problems in the field of cotton textiles on the basis of the guiding principles set out in the Preamble to this Arrangement.

2. Collect all useful data for this purpose.
3. At an early date, not later than 30 April 1962, make recommendations for such long-term solution.

B. The discussions and consultations to be undertaken by the Committee on the long-term problem shall be of the kind provided for by the Market Disruption Committee at the seventeenth session of the Contracting Parties. The Committee shall, as appropriate, from time to time report to this Committee and to Committee III of the Expansion of Trade Programme on progress made and on its findings.

PROGRAMME OF ACTION DIRECTED TOWARDS AN EXPANSION
OF INTERNATIONAL TRADE

The Contracting Parties
Decide:

1. To initiate immediate consideration of a co-ordinated programme of action directed to a substantial advance towards the attainment of the objectives of the General Agreement through the further reduction of barriers to the expansion of international trade. The programme shall embrace three principal topics, that is to say:
(a) the possibilities of further negotiations for the reduction of tariffs;
(b) problems arising out of the widespread use of non-tariff measures for the protection of agriculture, or in support of the maintenance of incomes of agricultural producers;
(c) other obstacles to the expansion of trade, with particular reference to the importance of maintaining and expanding the export earnings of the less developed countries.
2. In order to lay down the lines of action to be taken for the carrying out of the co-ordinated programme, to establish three committees under the following terms of reference.

Committee II

1. To assemble, in consultation with other competent international organizations, and in particular with the Food and Agriculture Organization of the United Nations, data regarding the use by contracting parties of non-tariff measures for the protection of agriculture or in support of incomes of agricultural producers, and the agricultural policies from which these measures derive. On the basis of such data and in consultation with the contracting parties concerned, to examine the effects of these measures adopted by individual contracting parties on international trade as a whole, and in particular on the trade in products entering importantly into international trade.
2. To consider, in the light of such data, the extent to which the existing rules of GATT and their application have proved inadequate to promote the expansion of international trade on a reciprocal and mutually advantageous basis as contemplated in Article I (revised), and to report on the steps that might appropriately be taken in the circumstances.
3. To suggest procedures for further consultations between all contracting parties on agricultural policies as they affect international trade.

DECISION ON TRADE AND ENVIRONMENT

Ministers...

Considering that there should not be, or need be, any policy contradiction between upholding and safeguarding an open, non-discriminatory and equitable multilateral trading system on the one hand, and acting for the protection of the environment, and the promotion of sustainable development on the other,

Desiring to coordinate the policies in the field of trade and environment, and this without exceeding the competence of the multilateral trading system, which is limited to trade policies and those trade-related aspects of environmental policies which may result in significant trade effects for its members,

Decide:

- to direct the first meeting of the General Council of the WTO to establish a Committee on Trade and Environment open to all members of the WTO to report to the first biennial meeting of the Ministerial Conference after the entry into force of the WTO when the work and terms of reference of the Committee will be reviewed, in the light of the recommendations of the Committee ...
- that within these terms of reference, and with the aim of making international trade and environmental policies mutually supportive, the Committee will initially address the following matters, in relation to which any relevant issue may be raised:
- the relationship between the provisions of the multilateral trading system and trade measures for environmental purposes, including those pursuant to multilateral environmental agreements;
- the relationship between environmental policies relevant to trade and environmental measures with significant trade effects and the provisions of the multilateral trading system;
- the relationship between the provisions of the multilateral trading system and:
  (a) charges and taxes for environmental purposes;
  (b) requirements for environmental purposes relating to products, including standards and technical regulations, packaging, labelling and recycling;
- the provisions of the multilateral trading system with respect to the transparency of trade measures used for environmental purposes and environmental measures and requirements which have significant trade effects;
- the relationship between the dispute settlement mechanisms in the multilateral trading system and those found in multilateral environmental agreements;
- the effect of environmental measures on market access, especially in relation to developing countries, in particular to the least developed among them, and environmental benefits of removing trade restrictions and distortions;
- the issue of exports of domestically prohibited goods,

that the Committee on Trade and Environment will consider the work programme envisaged in the Declaration on Trade in Services and the Environment and the relevant provisions of the Agreement on Trade-Related Aspects of Intellectual Property Rights as an integral part of its work, within the above terms of reference ...

Notes

INTRODUCTION

1 See Marrakesh Agreement Establishing the World Trade Organization, in WTO, *The Legals Texts: The Results of the Uruguay Round of Multilateral Trade Negotiations* (Cambridge: Cambridge University Press, 1999) (hereinafter *The Results of the Uruguay Round*), pp. 3–14. For a general introduction to the WTO, see Mitsuo Matsushita, Thomas J. Schoenbaum and Petros Mavriodis, *The World Trade Organization: Law, Practice, and Policy* (Oxford: Oxford University Press, 2003).

2 In addition, there is the importance of international trade for global economic growth and prosperity and a growing recognition that international trade law and the institutions governing international trade are part of the broader corpus of international law and thus that they have a role to play in a world where international law helps to structure interstate relations. Moreover, since its creation in 1995 the WTO has assumed an increasingly heavy workload. See James Bacchus, 'Groping Toward Grotius: The WTO and the International Rule of Law', *Harvard International Law Journal*, Vol. 44, No. 2, 2003, pp. 533–50, at p. 540.

3 See General Agreement on Tariffs and Trade (GATT 1947) in *The Results of the Uruguay Round*, pp. 423–92.

4 For an overview of this process see Paul Demaret, 'The Metamorphoses of the GATT: From the Havana Charter to the World Trade Organization', *Columbia Journal of Transnational Law*, Vol. 34, No. 1, 1995, pp. 123–71, and S.P. Shukla, *From GATT to WTO and Beyond*, No. 195 (Helsinki: World Institute for Development Economics Research, United Nations University, 2000).

5 See John H. Jackson, 'The WTO "Constitution" and Proposed Reforms: Seven Mantras Revisited', *Journal of International Economic Law*, Vol. 4, No. 1, 2001, pp. 67–78, and John H. Jackson, *The World Trade Organization: Constitution and Jurisprudence* (London: Royal Institute of International Affairs/Pinter, 1998).

6 See below for an outline of the WTO's institutional framework.

7 The agreements are reprinted in *The Results of the Uruguay Round*.

8 Understanding on Rules and Procedures Governing the Settlement of Disputes. Ibid., pp. 354–79. For an analysis of the DSU and its impact, see David Palmeter and Petros C. Mavriodis, *Dispute Settlement in the World Trade Organization – Practice and Procedure* (The Hague: Kluwer Law International, 1999).

9 See the Trade Policy Review Mechanism in the *Results of the Uruguay Round*, pp. 380–82. The TPRM is analysed in the following: Petros C. Mavriodis, 'Surveillance

Schemes: The GATT's New Trade Policy Review Mechanism', *Michigan Journal of International Law*, Vol. 13, No. 2, 1992, pp. 374–414; Donald B. Keesing, *Improving Trade Policy Reviews in the World Trade Organization* (Washington, DC: Institute for International Economics, 1998); and Sam Laird, 'The WTO's Trade Policy Review Mechanism: From Through the Looking Glass', *The World Economy*, Vol. 22, No. 6, August 1999, pp. 741–64.

10 This is the effect of the Single Undertaking. But see Chandrakant Patel, *Single Undertaking: A Straitjacket or Variable Geometry?* (Geneva: South Centre, 2003) in which he argues that the Single Undertaking is neither a binding norm nor a new regime under the WTO system.

11 This is an outcome of the change in GATT/WTO rules from consensus to block a panel report to consensus to adopt a report. See DSU, Article 16 (4) in *The Results of the Uruguay Round*.

12 Even when there is a dispute about whether the WTO is a fully-fledged supranational organization, the rapid expansion of its remit to include areas such as services and intellectual property and its 'relative autonomy from and power over governments' is indicative of its role in global trade governance. See Jan Aart Scholte, Robert O'Brien and Marc Williams, *The WTO and Civil Society* (Coventry, UK: Centre for the Study of Globalisation and Regionalisation, University of Warwick, 1998) p. 2.

13 See DSU, Article 17 (1) in *The Results of the Uruguay Round*.

14 See Robert Hudec, 'The GATT Legal System: A Diplomat's Jurisprudence', *Journal of World Trade Law*, Vol. 4, No. 5, 1970, p. 615 and Arie Reich, 'From Diplomacy to Law: The Juridicization of International Trade Relations', *Northwestern Journal of International Law and Business*, Vol. 17, No. 2/3, 1997, p. 775.

15 The initial perception of the GATT was that it had a 'flimsy' constitutional basis. This is because it was rooted in an agreement that was not supposed to be the 'central organizing mechanism' for the world trading system and also because owing to grandfather rights, the GATT's rules were subject to prior national legislation. This weak constitutional basis was worsened further by the weaknesses inherent in the GATT bureaucracy, the proliferation of side agreements, which were outside the GATT's structure, and the consequences arising from the GATT's voting structure. See John H. Jackson, 'The Crumbling Institutions of the Liberal Trade System', *Journal of World Trade Law*, Vol. 12, No. 2, 1978, pp. 93–106, at p. 96.

16 See Gail E. Evans, *Lawmaking under the Trade Constitution: A Study in Legislating by the World Trade Organization*, Studies in Transnational Economic Law (Boston, MA: Kluwer Law International, 2000), pp. 49–50.

17 See Agreement Establishing the WTO, Article XVI (4) in *The Results of the Uruguay Round*.

18 See Chakravarthi Raghavan, *Recolonization: GATT, Uruguay Round and the Third World* (London: Zed Books, 1990/Penang, Malaysia: Third World Network, 2000); Lori Wallach and Michelle Sforza, *Whose Trade Organization? Corporate Globalization and the Erosion of Democracy: an Assessment of the World Trade Organization* (Washington, DC: Public Citizen, 1999) and Susan Hainsworth, 'Sovereignty, Economic Integration and the World Trade Organization', *Osgoode Hall Law Journal*, Vol. 33, No. 3, 1995, pp. 584–622.

19 See John H. Jackson, 'The Great 1994 Sovereignty Debate: United States Acceptance and Implementation of the Uruguay Round Results', *Columbia Journal of Transnational Law*, Vol. 36, No. 1, 1997, pp. 157–88.

20 See Robert Hudec, *Developing Countries in the GATT Legal System* (London: Gower for Trade Policy Research Centre, 1987); Will Martin and L. Alan Winters (eds), *The Uruguay Round and the Developing Economies* (Washington, DC: World Bank, 1995); T.N. Srinivasan, *Developing Countries and the Multilateral System: From the GATT to the Uruguay Round and the Future* (Boulder, CO: Westview Press, 1998); Diana Tussie and David Glover (eds), *The Developing Countries in World Trade: Policies and Bargaining Strategies* (Boulder, CO: Lynne Rienner, 1993); Peter Gallagher, *Guide to the WTO and Developing Countries* (The Hague: Kluwer Law International, 2000); Amritar Narlikar, *International Trade and Developing Countries: Coalitions in GATT and WTO* (London: Routledge, 2003); and John Whalley (ed.) *The Uruguay Round and Beyond: The Final Report from the Ford Foundation Supported Project on Developing Countries and the Global Trading System* (London: Macmillan, 1989).

21 The GATT/WTO codes and agreements began as rules on non-tariff barriers that came to prominence at the end of the Toyko Round. Initially, most of the signatories to them were the industrialized GATT members. However, at the end of the Uruguay Round most of these agreements were multilateralized. Generally speaking, compared to other areas of GATT/WTO scholarship, there has not been that much research on the GATT/WTO committees. For studies of note, see Gregory C. Schaffer, 'The World Trade Organization under Challenge: Democracy and the Law and Politics of the WTO's Treatment of Trade and Environment Matters', *Harvard Environmental Law Review*, Vol. 25, No. 1, 2001, pp. 1–93; Richard Eglin, 'Surveillance of Balance-of-Payments Measures in the GATT', *The World Economy*, Vol. 10, 1987, pp. 1–26; Jennifer Schultz, 'The GATT/WTO Committee on Trade and the Environment – Toward Environmental Reform', *American Journal of International Law*, Vol. 89, No. 2, 1995, pp. 423–39; and K. Kristine Dunn, 'The Textiles Monitoring Body: Can it Bring Textiles Trade into GATT?', *Minnesota Journal of Global Trade*, Vol. 7, No. 1, 1998, pp. 123–55.

22 See Anne O. Krueger, *Developing Countries and the Next Round of Multilateral Trade Negotiations* (Washington DC: World Bank, 1999), and Michel Camdessus, 'Bolstering Market Access of Developing Countries in a Globalized World', 6 July 1998, <*http://www.imf.org/external/np/speeches/ 1998/070698.htm*>. On DCs and the GATT/WTO antidumping system, see Kofi Oteng Kufuor, 'The Developing Countries and the Shaping of GATT/WTO Antidumping Law', *Journal of World Trade*, Vol. 32, December 1998, pp. 167–96; Brian Hindley and Patrick Messerlin, *Antidumping Industrial Policy: Legalized Protectionism in the WTO and What to Do About It* (Washington, DC: American Enterprise Institute Press, 1996); P.K.M. Tharakan, *The Problem of Anti-Dumping and Developing Country Exports* (Helsinki: World Institute for Development Economics Research, United Nations University, 2000); and Inge Nora Neufeld, *Anti-Dumping and Countervailing Procedures: Use or Abuse? Implications for Developing Countries* (Geneva: UNCTAD, 2001), pp. 14–15.

23 See *WTO Annual Report* (Geneva: WTO, 2003), p. 23.

24 Idem.

25 Idem. India has initiated 75 investigations and Argentina has initiated 26. The United States leads with 76 investigations and the EC is third with 29. For an examination of this development, see Kofi Oteng Kufuor, *The Growing Problem of Intra-LDC Antidumping Actions in World Trade* (London: University of East London, Eastlaw Press, 2001/2).

26 See *WTO Annual Report* (2003), p. 23. India has initiated 248 antidumping investi-

gations since 1995 and Argentina has initiated 166. The US has been responsible for 257 investigations and the EC for 247.

27 Idem. China has been investigated 53 times, Taiwan and South Korea 19 times each and Indonesia and Thailand 16 times each.

28 See Krueger, 'Developing Countries in the Next Round of Multilateral Trade Negotiations', p. 6.

29 Idem.

30 See the following: *A Study on Cotton Textiles* (Geneva: GATT, 1966), p. 7; Herbert Kisch, *From Domestic Manufacture to Industrial Revolution: The Case of the Rhineland Textile Districts* (New York: Oxford University Press, 1989), pp. 21–2; Young-Il Park and Kym Anderson, 'The Rise and Demise of Textiles and Clothing in Economic Development: The Case of Japan', in Michael Smitka (ed.), *The Textile Industry and the Rise of the Japanese Economy* (New York: Garland Publishing, 1998), pp. 165–82. The establishment of a textile industry, based on cotton, and to some extent on wool, was the starting point in the industrialization of most of the industrially advanced countries. The demand for clothing as a basic need created a natural mass market, and the logical consequence of the mechanization of spindles and looms was the transfer of spinning and weaving from homes and handicraft shops to factories using mechanical power, with the object of achieving production on a large scale. For instance, Japan's transformation from an agrarian to an industrialized country was determined to a significant extent by its comparative advantage in the world trade in textiles. From the 1870s to the 1930s the contribution of textiles and clothing to Japan's economy grew steadily so that in the 1920s they accounted for 30 per cent of manufacturing value added and approximately 60 per cent of both industrial employment and exports of manufactures. Given that the DCs are the main exporters of clothing, institutions for the regulation of international trade in this sector of the world economy are extremely important to them.

31 For the DCs and the GATT/WTO regulation of trade in agriculture, see Kele Onyejekwe, 'GATT Agriculture and Developing Countries', *Hamline Law Review*, Vol. 17, 1993, pp. 77–153; Bernard Hoekman, *Reducing Agricultural Tariffs versus Domestic Support: What's More Important for Developing Countries?*, World Bank Policy Research Working Paper No. 2918 (Washington, DC: World Bank, 2003); Merlinda D. Ingco, *Agricultural Trade Liberalization in a New Trade Round: Perspectives of Developing Countries and Transition Economies*, World Bank Policy Research Working Paper No. 418 (Washington, DC: World Bank, 2000); Melaku Geboye Desta, *The Law of International Trade in Agricultural Products from GATT 1947 to WTO Agreement on Agriculture* (The Hague: Kluwer Law International, 2002); and Carmen G. Gonzalez, 'Institutionalizing Inequality: The WTO Agreement on Agriculture, Food Security and Developing Countries', *Columbia Journal of Environmental Law*, Vol. 27, No. 2, 2002, pp. 433–90.

32 See Ulrike Grote, *Implications and Challenges of Liberalized Agricultural Markets for Developing Countries: An Institutional Perspective* (Bonn: Centre for Development Research, 2001), p. 4.

33 See Paul Gibson, John Vainio, Daniel Whitley and Mary Bohman, *Profiles of Tariffs in Global Agricultural Market*, Agricultural Economic Report No. 796 (Washington, DC: US Department of Agriculture, 2001), p. 35. This is, in part, a reflection of the Special and Differential Treatment provided to the DCs, particularly the flexibility provided on ceiling bindings and lower reduction commitments.

34 Idem. As results indicate for the US, the EU and Japan, one-quarter of all tariff lines in these countries are duty free, involving a large number of products of export interest to DCs. In addition, the actual tariff rates these countries apply to imports from individual DCs are often lower than the most-favoured-nation rate would indicate. This is due to the existence of the Generalized System of Preferences, which provides for lower rates for selected countries and commodities, and to other concessions afforded through various preferential trading arrangements.

35 See Gary P. Sampson, *Trade, Environment, and the WTO: The Post-Seattle Agenda* (Washington, DC: Overseas Development Council, 2000); Diane Tussie (ed.), *The Environment in International Trade Negotiations: Developing Country Stakes* (Basingstoke: Macmillan in association with the International Development Research Centre (Ottawa), 2000); and Beatrice Chaytor and Mathias Wolkewitz, 'Participation and Priorities: An Assessment of Developing Country Concerns in the Trade/Environment Interface', *Review of European Community and International Environmental Law*, Vol. 6, July 1997, pp. 157–62.

CHAPTER I

1 For an introduction to Realism in international relations, see E.H. Carr, *The Twenty Years' Crisis, 1919–1939: An Introduction to the Study of International Relations* (London and New York: Torchbooks, 1964); Hans J. Morgenthau, *Politics among Nations: the Struggle for Power and Peace* (New York: Alfred A. Knopf, 5th edn, 1973); and Robert Gilpin, *U.S. Power and the Multinational Corporation: The Political Economy of Foreign Direct Investment* (New York: Basic Books, 1975).

2 For a discussion of anarchy in international relations, see Hedley Bull, *The Anarchical Society: A Study of World Order in Politics* (New York: Columbia University Press, 2nd edn, 1977).

3 See Stephen Krasner, 'Structural Causes and Regime Consequences: Regimes as Intervening Variables', *International Organization*, Vol. 36, No. 2, 1982, pp. 185–205, at p. 186.

4 See Anne-Marie Slaughter, 'Liberal International Relations Theory and International Economic Law', *American University Journal of International Law and Policy*, Vol. 10, No. 2, 1995, pp. 717–43, at p. 725.

5 Ibid., p. 727.

6 See Anne-Marie Slaughter Burley, 'International Law and International Relations Theory: A Dual Agenda', *American Journal of International Law*, Vol. 87, No. 2, 1993, pp. 205–39. The author is seen as possibly the leading exponent of a Liberal approach to understanding international relations.

7 See Andrew Moravcsik, 'Taking Preferences Seriously: A Liberal Theory of International Politics', *International Organization*, Vol. 51, No. 4, 1997, pp. 513–53, at p. 517. Moravcsik identifies four types of Liberal theory: Commercial Liberalism, which stresses the ways in which transnational economic interdependence and externalities shape state behaviour; Republican Liberalism, which emphasizes the ways in which different types of domestic governing institutions structure the interactions of social groups, thereby determining which configuration of social interests and ideas will most likely shape state preferences; Regulatory Liberalism, which stresses the ways in which international institutions and organizations shape the behaviour of states; and Sociological or Ideational Liberalism, which emphasizes the ways in which ideas, values, norms, and practices shape the behaviour of states.

8 See Slaughter, 'Liberal International Relations Theory and International Economic Law', p. 728.

9 Ibid., p. 729.

10 This is one instance in which Realists and Liberals agree about the nature of inter-state relations. The differences arise in how to manage the anarchical international system.

11 See Slaughter, 'Liberal International Relations Theory and International Economic Law', p. 729.

12 See Adam Smith, *An Inquiry into the Nature and Causes of the Wealth of Nations* (London: Everyman's Library, 1776, 1991).

13 For an introduction to the Prisoner's Dilemma see Robert M. Axelrod, *The Evolution of Cooperation* (New York: Basic Books, 1984). See Kenneth W. Abbot, 'The Trading Nation's Dilemma: The Functions of the Law of International Trade', *Harvard International Law Journal*, Vol. 26, No. 2, 1985, pp. 501–32.

14 See Harold Hongju Koh, 'The Legal Markets of International Trade: A Perspective on the Proposed United States–Canada Free Trade Agreement', *Yale Journal of International Law*, Vol. 12, No. 2, 1987, pp. 193–249, at p. 196; and Abbott, 'The Trading Nation's Dilemma'.

15 The GATT/WTO does not explicitly define a DC. GATT Article XVIII: 1 notes merely that a developing country is one whose economy can support only low standards of living and is in the early stages of development. For a discussion of the problem of defining a DC, see Gugliemo Verdirame, 'The Definition of Developing Countries under GATT and other International Law', *German Yearbook of International Law*, Vol. 39, 1996, pp. 164–97.

16 See Koh, 'The Legal Markets of International Trade', p. 196. This is the application of social choice theory to the study of international trade decision-making. Social choice theory is the formal study of collective decision procedures, i.e. of aggregating combinations of individual preferences into a social preference relation. Individual preferences are transformed into collective decisions by voting, coalition-formation etc. For an introduction to social choice theory, see Kenneth J. Arrow, *Social Choice and Individual Values* (New York: Wiley, 2nd edn, 1963).

17 See Koh, 'The Legal Markets of International Trade', p. 198. Institutionalism stresses the importance of formal laws, customs and their enforcement for policy outcomes. For a seminal analysis of the role institutions play in shaping policy outcomes, see Douglass C. North, *Institutions, Institutional Change, and Economic Performance* (Cambridge: Cambridge University Press, 1990).

18 See Marrakesh Agreement Establishing the World Trade Organization, Article IV, paras 1–5, in *The Results of the Uruguay Round* for structure described in this and the next paragraph.

19 See Terence P. Stewart (ed.), *The GATT Uruguay Round: A Negotiating History 1986–1992* (Deventer, The Netherlands: Kluwer Law International, 1993), p. 1908.

20 Ibid., note 87.

21 Ibid., pp. 1907–8.

22 See Axelrod, *The Evolution of Cooperation*, p. 3.

23 See Ronald Coase, 'The Problem of Social Cost', *Journal of Law and Economics*, Vol. 3, No. 1, 1960, pp. 1–44, and Ronald Coase, 'The Nature of the Firm', *Economica*, Vol. 4, 1937, pp. 386–405.

24 See Beth V. Yarbrough and Robert M. Yarbrough, 'Institutions for the Governance

of Opportunism in International Trade', *Journal of Law, Economics and Organization*, Vol. 3, No. 1, 1987, pp. 129–39. Transaction cost economics tries to explain the existence of firms in terms of market failures, which Coase thought were due to the high costs of exchanging or transacting in markets. See Coase, 'The Problem of Social Cost' and Coase, 'The Nature of the Firm'.

25 See Yarbrough and Yarbrough, 'Institutions for the Governance of Opportunism in International Trade'.

26 See Terry M. Moe, 'Political Institutions: The Neglected Side of the Story', *Journal of Law, Economics and Organization*, special issue, Vol. 6, 1990, pp. 213–53, at p. 213.

27 See Roland Vaubel, 'A Public Choice View of International Organization', in Roland Vaubel and Thomas D. Willett (eds), *The Political Economy of International Organization: A Public Choice Approach* (Boulder, CO: Westview Press, 1991), pp. 27–45, at pp. 38–9.

28 See Protocol Amending the General Agreement on Tariffs and Trade to Introduce a Part IV on Trade and Development, *GATT BISD, 13th Supplement*, pp. 2–10. Under Article 4, the contracting parties are to enhance market access for DC exports.

29 Ibid., p. 75. The WTO is, arguably, reinforcing its role as a redistributive institution. See Peter M. Gerhart, 'Reflections on the WTO Doha Ministerial: Slow Transformations: The WTO as a Distributive Organization', *American University International Law Review*, Vol. 17, No. 5, 2002, pp. 1045–95.

30 See Ernst-Ulrich Petersmann, *The GATT/WTO Dispute Settlement System: International Law, International Organization and Dispute Settlement* (London: Kluwer Law International, 1997), p. 5.

31 See Jagdish Bhagwati, *Protectionism* (Cambridge, MA: MIT Press, 1988), and Sima Lieberman, *The Economic and Political Roots of the New Protectionism* (Lanham, MD: Rowman and Littlefield, 1988).

32 On this see Patrick McNutt, *The Economics of Public Choice* (Cheltenham, UK: Edward Elgar, 2002), and James M. Buchanan and Gordon Tullock, *The Calculus of Consent: Logical Foundations of Constitutional Democracy* (Ann Arbor, MI: University of Michigan Press, 1962).

33 See Agreement on Safeguards, in *The Results of the Uruguay Round*, pp. 315–24.

34 The Committee on Safeguards is established under Article 13 (1) of the Agreement on Safeguards.

35 See Agreement on Subsidies and Countervailing Measures, in *The Results of the Uruguay Round*, pp. 264–97. The Committee on Subsidies and Countervailing Measures is established under Article 24 (1).

36 Ibid., Article 9.

37 See Ian R. McNeil, 'Contracts: Adjustment of Long-Term Economic Relations Under Classical, Neoclassical and Relational Contract Law', *Northwestern University Law Review*, Vol. 72, No. 6, 1978, pp. 854–906.

38 On opportunism in international relations, see Yarbrough and Yarbrough, 'Institutions for the Governance of Opportunism in International Trade'.

39 'Bounded rationality' designates rational choice that takes into account decision-makers' and negotiators' cognitive limitations. Bounded rationality is a central theme in behavioural economics. See Herbert Simon, 'A Behavioural Model of Rational Choice', *Quarterly Journal of Economics*, Vol. 69, No. 1, 1955, pp. 99–118. On bounded rationality and interstate bargaining see John Odell, *Negotiating the World Economy* (Ithaca, NY: Cornell University Press, 2000).

40 See Duncan Snidal, 'Political Economy and International Institutions', *International Review of Law and Economics*, Vol. 16, No. 1, 1996, pp. 121–37, at p. 127.

41 See Jarle Trondal, *Why Europeanisation Happens: The Transformative Power of EU Committees*, Arena Working Paper 02/3 (Oslo: Norwegian Institute for Studies in Research and Higher Education, 2002), p. 2.

42 Ibid., p. 4.

43 Idem.

CHAPTER 2

1 See Hudec, *Developing Countries in the GATT Legal System*. The size of developed countries' economies and their share of world trade reinforced this control. See Alice Landau, 'Analyzing International Economic Negotiations: Towards a Synthesis of Approaches', *International Negotiation*, Vol. 5, No. 1, 2000, pp. 1–19, at pp. 10–11. Given the Single Undertaking, DC delegations are aware that decisions arrived at even informally in the WTO could eventually lead to the acceptance of new obligations. It is thus not sound policy for them to be left out of the decision-making process.

2 On the evolution of the GATT system, see Robert Hudec, *Enforcing International Trade Law: The Evolution of the Modern GATT Legal System* (Salem, NH: Butterworth, 1993). For the emergence of the codes as part of the GATT system, see Gilbert R. Winham, *International Trade and the Tokyo Round Negotiations* (Princeton, NJ: Princeton University Press, 1986). For the codes, see the Annexes to the Marakesh Agreement Establishing the World Trade Organization. For the case law of the GATT/WTO, see Pierre Pescatore, William J. Davey and Andreas F. Lowenfeld (eds), *Handbook of WTO/GATT Dispute Settlement* (Irvington-on-Hudson, New York, and Transnational Publishers/The Hague: Kluwer Law International, 2 vols, 1996), and also the WTO's website (*www.wto.org*).

3 See Trondal, *Why Europeanisation Happens*, and Jeffrey T. Checkel, *Why Comply? Constructivism, Social Norms and the Study of International Institutions*, Arena Working Paper 99/24, *http://www.arena.uio.no/ publications/wp99_24.htm*, p. 13 (visited on 7 October 2001). The page number cited is based on the copy on the website.

4 Jacob Viner was the first to note this in his work on dumping. See Jacob Viner, *Dumping: A Problem in International Trade* (New York: Kelley, 1923). For recent research on dumping as a problem, see John H. Jackson, *The World Trading System: Law and Policy in International Economic Relations* (Cambridge, MA: MIT Press, 1989), pp. 217–47; and Kufuor, *The Growing Problem of Intra-LDC Antidumping Actions in World Trade*.

5 See the GATT Treaty, Article 6 (1) in *The Results of the Uruguay Round*, pp. 423–92.

6 See Preamble to Agreement on Implementation of Article VI of the General Agreement on Tariffs and Trade in *GATT BISD 15th Supplement*, pp. 24–35. (Reprinted, in part, in the Appendix to this volume.)

7 Ibid., Article 17.

8 Idem.

9 For an explanation of this, see Kofi Oteng Kufuor, 'The Developing Countries and the Shaping of GATT/WTO Antidumping Law', *Journal of World Trade*, Vol. 32, No. 6, December 1998, pp. 167–96, at pp. 170–74.

10 See 'Second Report of the Committee on Anti-Dumping Practices', *GATT BISD 18th Supplement*, pp. 42–4, at p. 44; and 'Fourth Report of the Committee on Anti-

Dumping Practices', *GATT BISD 19th Supplement*, pp. 15–18, at p. 18.

11 In 1967 the CADP's members were Belgium, Canada, Czechoslovakia, Denmark, the European Economic Community, Finland, France, the Federal Republic of Germany, Greece, Italy, Luxembourg, the Netherlands, Norway, Sweden, Switzerland, the United Kingdom, the United States and Yugoslavia. See 'Report of the Committee on Antidumping Practices', *GATT BISD 17th Supplement*, pp. 43–6, at p. 43. In 1978, as the Tokyo Round was drawing to a close, the following states, none of which were DCs, had signed the 1979 Antidumping Code and had become members of the 1979 CADP: Australia, Austria, Greece, Hungary, Japan, Malta, Poland, Portugal and Spain. See '10th Report of the Committee on Antidumping Practices', *GATT BISD, 25th Supplement*, pp. 17–28, at p. 17.

12 See Robert C. Ellikson, 'A Hypothesis of Wealth-Maximizing Norms: Evidence from the Whaling Industry', *Journal of Law, Economics and Organization*, Vol. 5, No. 1, 1989, pp. 83–97, at p. 84.

13 See Lars Anell and Brigitta Nygren, *The Developing Countries and the World Economic Order* (London: Pinter, 1980), especially pp. 15–60, and Harold B. Malmgrem, 'Trade Policy of Developed Countries for the Next Decade', in Jagdish N. Bhagwati (ed.), *The New International Economic Order: The North–South Debate* (Cambridge, MA: MIT Press, 1977), pp. 219–35.

14 This section draws to some extent on Kufuor, 'The Developing Countries and the Shaping of GATT/WTO Antidumping Law', pp. 173–4.

15 Towards the end of the Tokyo Round it was becoming obvious that the aggressive export offensive of the newly industrializing countries was beginning to have serious implications for DCs, as they became targets of antidumping actions by the European Union, Canada, the United States and Japan. This development led to the beginning of a change in attitude by some of the DCs towards the GATT as a whole. Ibid., p. 177. As a matter of fact, on the eve of the Tokyo Round it was noted that measures were afoot to bring the DCs into the orbit of the GATT Antidumping Code. The 1967 CADP observed that a special working party was exploring the question of adherence to the code by the DCs. See '4th Report of the Committee on Anti-Dumping Practices', *GATT BISD 19th Supplement*, p. 18.

16 See 'Statement by the Representative of Egypt', GATT Doc. No. MTN/NTM/W/143 (10 March 1978), and 'Antidumping Duties', GATT Doc. No. MTN/INF/30 (30 June 1979), cited in Terence P. Stewart (ed.), *The GATT Uruguay Round: A Negotiating History 1986–1992* (Deventer, The Netherlands: Kluwer Law International, 1993), p. 1454, notes 456 and 457. Included in the definitions of dumping under the 1967 Antidumping Code was price discrimination between markets. See 1967 Antidumping Code, Article 2 (a).

17 See Stewart, *The GATT Uruguay Round*, p. 1454.

18 See Agreement on Implementation of Article VI of the GATT, *GATT BISD 26th Supplement*, pp. 171–8 (hereinafter the 1979 Antidumping Code).

19 Below-cost sales had been a feature of antidumping laws since the 1920s when Canada extended its antidumping regulations to cover sales below the cost of production with a reasonable allowance for production overheads and profits. See J. Michael Finger and Sumana Dhar, *Do Rules Control Power? GATT Articles and Arrangements in the Uruguay Round*, World Bank Policy Research Working Paper No. 818 (Washington, DC: World Bank, 1992), p. 14. The US followed suit as a consequence of its tariff reductions and the increased pressure by business for trade

remedy action. Ibid., pp. 14–15. Although the 1967 Antidumping Code allowed other calculations of home-market price (in addition to price discrimination between home and overseas markets), it was never specific on whether this applied to below-cost sales. Ibid., pp.15–16. However, during the Tokyo Round, the US, the EC, Australia and Canada came to an agreement which in effect signified that the interpretation of Article 2 (4) of the new (1979) antidumping code would mean below-cost sales. Ibid., p. 16.

20 See 1979 Antidumping Code, Article 2 (4).

21 Ibid., Article 14. (See Appendix of this book for this Article and Article 15.)

22 Ibid., Article 14 (1).

23 Ibid., Article 14 (4).

24 Idem.

25 Ibid., Article 15.

26 See 1967 Antidumping Code, Article 15.

27 Ibid., Article 16.

28 Ibid., Article 14 (3).

29 On the exploitation of antidumping actions by national interests seeking shelter from foreign competition, see Katsuyuki Yano, 'Thirty Years of Being a Respondent in Antidumping Proceedings – Abuse of Economic Relief Can Have a Negative Impact on Competition Policy', *Journal of World Trade*, Vol. 33, No. 5, October 1999, pp. 31–47, and J. Michael Finger, *The Origins and Evolution of Antidumping Regulation*, World Bank Policy Research Working Paper No. 783 (Washington, DC: World Bank, 1991).

30 See Agreement on Technical Barriers to Trade, Article 14 and Annex 3, in *GATT BISD 26th Supplement*, pp. 8–32; Agreement on Government Procurement, Article VII, in ibid., pp. 33–55; Agreement on Interpretation and Application of Articles VI, XVI and XXII, Articles 12, 13, 17, and 18, in ibid., pp. 56–83; Agreement on Interpretation of Article VII, Article 20, in ibid., pp. 116–50 and Annex III; Agreement on Import Licensing Procedures Article 4, in ibid., pp. 154–61; and Agreement on Trade in Civil Aircraft, Article 8, in ibid., pp. 162–70.

31 See 1979 Antidumping Code, Article 15 (2).

32 Ibid., Article 15 (3).

33 Ibid., 15 (5).

34 See GATT, *The Results of the Uruguay Round*, Article XXV (1).

35 Ibid., Article XXV (7).

36 See Committee on Antidumping Practices, 'Decision of 5 May 1980', para. 2 in *GATT BISD 27th Supplement*, pp. 16–18. (See also the Appendix of this volume.)

37 Olivier Long, *Law and its Limitations in the GATT Multilateral Trade System* (Dordrecht, The Netherlands: Martinus Nijhoff, 1985), p. 78.

38 Idem.

39 For DC participation in the GATT dispute settlement system at the time see, Kofi Oteng Kufuor, 'From the GATT to the WTO: The Developing Countries and the Reform of the Procedures for the Settlement of International Trade Disputes', *Journal of World Trade*, Vol. 31, No. 5, October 1997, pp. 117–47, and Pretty Elizabeth Kuruvila, 'Developing Countries and the GATT/WTO Dispute Settlement Mechanism', *Journal of World Trade*, Vol. 31, No. 6, December 1997, pp. 171–208.

40 See US General Accounting Office, *International Trade: Use of the GATT Antidumping Code* (Washington, DC: US General Accounting Office, 1990).

41 See Committee on Anti-Dumping Practices, Decision 5 May 1980, p. 17, para. 1 (ii).

42 Ibid., para. (iii). The decision of 1980 was given effect when the 1979 CADP acknowledged that Brazil's administrative structures were such that it required an extension of the GATT-mandated time-period to establish an administrative structure and set up administrative procedures in order to implement its antidumping legislation. See 'Decision of 20/22 October 1980', in *GATT BISD 28th Supplement*, p. 26. (See the Appendix of this book.)

43 On Special and Differential Treatment for the DCs in the GATT, see Hudec, *Developing Countries and the GATT Legal System*; Constantine Michalopolous, *The Role of Special and Differential Treatment for Developing Countries in GATT and the World Trade Organization* (Washington, DC: World Bank, 2000); and Edwini Kessie, 'Enforceability of the Legal Provisions Relating to Special and Differential Treatment under the WTO Agreements', *Journal of World Intellectual Property*, Vol. 3, No.6, 2000, pp. 955–75.

44 See Kufuor, 'The Developing Countries and the Shaping of GATT/WTO Antidumping Law', pp. 176–7. In *Cotton Yarn Imports from Brazil*, there was also an attempt to clarify the meaning of Special and Differential Treatment. Brazil thus sought to crystallize into 'hard law' in the GATT system this principle, which was seen as subject to the discretion of developed-country contracting parties. Despite its insertion in the various GATT/WTO agreements as to the special concessions granted to DC contracting parties, the developed countries have always held that Special and Differential Treatment for DCs is largely for the developed countries to decide and that it is not enforceable under the GATT/WTO. In effect, Special and Differential Treatment amounts to nothing more than the GATT/WTO urging the developed countries to adopt 'best practices' when dealing with DCs. Thus as far as GATT antidumping law was concerned, Brazil's submission was novel in that it was trying to assert that Article 13 could be construed as a binding provision. (Article 13 of the 1979 Antidumping Agreement charged the developed-country parties to the 1979 Antidumping Code with giving due consideration to the status of DCs when deciding whether to apply antidumping measures under the Agreement.) Brazil's argument was that in imposing antidumping duties, the EC was in breach of Article 13 because it had not given due consideration to Brazil as a DC and that it had also failed to consider properly the constructive remedies put forward by Brazilian exporters. According to the Brazilian submission, the EC had certain minimum responsibilities under Article 13: Its investigating authority was to 'take due consideration of the submissions made orally and in writing; (2) the investigating authorities acknowledge receipt of and respond to the relevant written submissions; (3) the public determinations of the investigating authorities refer to relevant written submissions, and (4) the public determinations of the investigating authorities be properly reasoned with regard to the facts submitted in writing, i.e. that the relevant facts reasonably support the determinations of the investigating authority' ('European Economic Community – Imposition of Anti-Dumping Duties on Imports of Cotton Yarn from Brazil: Report of the Panel adopted by the Committee on Anti-Dumping Practices on 30 October 1995', *GATT BISD 42nd Supplement*). Brazil therefore contended that a breach of Article 13 would be established where it could be demonstrated that an investigating authority failed to have 'regard' to the special situation of a DC.

Rejecting Brazil's argument on the true meaning of Article 13, the panel established by the 1979 CADP took a restricted view of the wording of this provision.

In rendering this strict construction of Article 13, the panel noted that the words 'possibilities' of 'constructive remedies' and 'explored' suggested that the investigating authorities were not required to adopt constructive remedies merely because they were proposed.

45 See Greg Mastel, *Antidumping Laws and the U.S. Economy* (Armonk, NY: M.E. Sharpe, 1998), Chart 2.6, p. 36 (noting how Taiwan, South Korea and Brazil were ranked second, third and fifth respectively among the top 20 respondents in US antidumping cases between 1980 and 1989).

46 This case can be found at *www.worldtradelaw.net/reports/gattpanels/usadcement/pdf.*

47 See 'European Economic Community – Imposition of Anti-Dumping Duties on Imports of Cotton Yarn from Brazil', pp. 17–190.

48 The only other complaint involving a DC was 'Korea – Anti-Dumping Duties on Imports of Polyacetal Resins from the United States', *GATT BISD 40th Supplement*, pp. 205–314.

49 See Angelika Eymann and Ludger Schuknecht, *Antidumping Enforcement in the European Community*, World Bank Policy Research Working Paper No. 743 (Washington, DC: World Bank, 1991), Table 1, p. 21.

50 See Mark A. Dutz, *Enforcement of Canadian 'Unfair' Trade Laws: The Case for Competition Policies as an Antidote for Protection*, World Bank Policy Research Working Paper No. 776 (Washington, DC: World Bank, 1991), Table 7, p. 45.

51 Ibid., p. 24.

52 Idem.

53 As of 1990 only the following DCs were signatories to the 1979 Code: Brazil, Egypt, Hong Kong, India, Korea, Mexico, Pakistan and Singapore. See 'Report of the Committee on Antidumping Practices', *GATT BISD 37th Supplement*, pp. 297–301, at p. 298.

54 See Miguel Montana i Mora, 'A GATT with Teeth: Law Wins Over Politics in the Resolution of International Trade Disputes', *Columbia Journal of Transnational Law*, Vol. 31, No. 1, 1993, pp. 103–80.

55 On the use of the GATT dispute settlement procedures by the DCs, see Kufuor, 'From the GATT to the WTO', pp. 128–32.

56 This is the view held by most observers of the DCs and GATT antidumping issues. But for a critique of this, see Kufuor, 'The Developing Countries and the Shaping of GATT/WTO Antidumping Law', pp. 172–3.

57 See Kufuor, 'From the GATT to the WTO', pp. 121–31.

58 This was one of the concerns DCs had about relying on the GATT dispute settlement provisions. See United States International Trade Commission, *Review of the Effectiveness of Trade Dispute Settlement under the GATT and the Tokyo Round Agreements* (Washington, DC: United States International Trade Commission, 1985), p. 70.

59 Idem.

60 See Nigel Harris, *The End of the Third World: Newly Industrialising Countries and the Decline of an Ideology* (Harmondsworth: Penguin Books, 1986), p. 31.

61 Ibid., p. 47.

62 Ibid., p. 56.

63 Idem.

64 Ibid., p. 66.

65 See *Economic Survey of Singapore* (Singapore: Ministry of Trade and Industry, 1986), Chart 3.1, p. 25.

66 See Yin-Ping Ho, *Trade, Industrial Restructuring, and Development in Hong Kong* (London: Macmillan, 1992), Table 1.1, p. 11.

67 See Il Sakong, *Korea in the World Economy* (Washington, DC: Institute for International Economics, 1993), pp. 14–15.

68 See Jene K. Kwon, *The East Asian Model: An Exploration of Rapid Economic Growth in the Republic of Korean and Taiwan Province of China* (Geneva: United Nations Conference on Trade and Development, 1998).

69 See J. Michael Finger, *The Meaning of 'Unfair' in U.S. Import Policy*, World Bank Policy Research Working Paper No. 745 (Washington, DC: World Bank, 1991), p. 2.

70 Idem.

71 VERs result in welfare losses whenever they restrict industries accounting for significant shares of the exporter's economic activity or when they make use of particular and relatively immobile skills or physical capital. See Jaime de Melo and L. Alan Winters, *Do Exporters Gain from Voluntary Export Restraints?*, World Bank Policy Research Working Paper No. 326 (Washington, DC: World Bank, 1990), p. 2.

72 In 1984 the Director-General of the GATT stated that 'voluntary export restraints are clearly contrary to the present rules of the General Agreement and are only "outside the General Agreement" in the sense that governments have not brought them formally to the GATT for examination'. Cited in Edmund McGovern, *International Trade Regulation: GATT, The United States and the European Community* (Exeter, UK: Globefield Press, 1995), p. 298.

73 See Martin Wolf, 'Why Voluntary Export Restraints? An Historical Analysis', *The World Economy*, Vol. 12, No. 3, September 1989, pp. 273–91.

74 However, for the negative effects of VERs see de Melo and Winters, *Do Exporters Gain from Voluntary Export Restraints?*

75 The antidumping agreements have allowed for the acceptance of price undertakings in lieu of antidumping duties. For example, see 1979 Antidumping Code, Article 7. This practice is continued under the WTO. See WTO Antidumping Agreement, Article 8.

76 See Thomas J. Prusa, 'Why Are So Many Antidumping Petitions Withdrawn?', *Journal of International Economics*, Vol. 33, No. 1/2, 1992, pp. 1–20, at p. 2.

77 Ibid., pp. 16–17.

78 See P.K.M. Tharakan, 'The Political Economy of Anti-Dumping Undertakings in the European Communities', *European Economic Review*, Vol. 35, 1991, pp. 1341–59.

79 See Klaus Stegemann, *Price Undertakings to Settle Anti-Dumping Cases* (Montreal: Institute for Research on Public Policy, 1992), p. 31.

80 Ibid., pp. 13–15.

81 See Kufuor, 'The Developing Countries and the Shaping of GATT/WTO Antidumping Law', pp. 173–4.

82 Officially named the Arrangement regarding International Trade in Cotton Textiles, this document is referred to throughout the text as the Short-Term Arrangement. See *GATT BISD 10th Supplement*, pp. 18–23.

83 Ibid., p. 21. (For the PCTC, see the Appendix of this book.) Actually the first GATT committee to deal with the world trade in textiles was the Committee on Avoidance of Market Disruption (CAMD). The CAMD's functions included dealing with issues that impinged on textiles trade, namely the actual or probable sudden surge in exports from DCs to the markets of the developed countries. The CAMD was to facilitate consultation between exporters and importers concerned with this

disruption. See Avoidance of Market Disruption, Establishment of Committee Decision of 19 November 1960, para. II, in *GATT BISD 9th Supplement*, pp. 26–8. To achieve this objective, the CAMD was to consider the problems described in the report of the Secretariat on 'Restrictions and other measures relating to the problem of market disruption' and to suggest multilaterally acceptable solutions, consistent with the principles and objectives of the General Agreement, for those problems which, in the light of this consideration, appear to call for immediate action. Ibid., para. V (I). The CAMD was authorized to make appropriate arrangements for preparing a report on various economic, social and commercial factors underlying the problems considered by the Committee, and in particular the relevance to international trade of differences in the costs of various factors of production and marketing, including labour costs. In preparing its report the Committee is authorized to call on experts, both governmental and non-governmental, and to seek the cooperation of the International Labour Office. Ibid., Para II.

84 See *GATT BISD 10th Supplement*, p. 21.
85 See Long-Term Arrangement Regarding International Trade in Cotton Textiles, *GATT BISD 11th Supplement*, pp. 25–35.
86 Ibid., Article 8 (a). (For Article 8 of the CTC, see the Appendix of this volume.)
87 Idem.
88 Idem, Article 8 (b).
89 Idem, 8 (c).
90 Idem, Article 7 (d).
91 See *GATT BISD 9th Supplement*, p. 26. A GATT decision on market disruption was a precondition for the United States agreeing to the launch of the Kennedy Round. US decision-makers had to respond to their domestic textile and apparel industries' demand for restraints on cotton imports from the DCs. See William R. Cline, *The Future of World Trade in Textiles and Apparel* (Washington, DC: Institute for International Economics, 1987), pp. 10 and 147.
92 See Gary H. Perlow, 'The Multilateral Supervision of International Trade: Has the Textiles Experiment Worked?', *American Journal of International Law*, Vol. 75, No. 1, 1981, pp. 93–133, at p. 99.
93 See First Review of the Operation of the Long-Term Arrangement, *GATT BISD 12th Supplement*, pp. 66–72. The DCs noted that strict conformity by importing countries with the terms of the LTA was easily avoided, as the powers of judgment and decision on market disruption were in the hands of the importing countries. Ibid., p. 67.
94 Idem.
95 Ibid., Article 8 (2).
96 Ibid., Article 7 (3).
97 See Niels Blokker, *International Regulation of World Trade in Textiles: Lessons for Practice: A Contribution to Theory* (Dordrecht, The Netherlands: Martinus Nijhoff, 1989), p. 141.
98 See Overseas Development Institute, *The Textile Trade, Developing Countries and the Multi-Fibre Arrangements* (1976), p. 2, cited in Perlow, 'The Multilateral Supervision of International Trade', p. 100.
99 See Arrangement Regarding International Trade in Textiles, *GATT BISD 21st Supplement*, pp. 3–19.
100 See Bernard Hoekman and Michel Kostecki, *The Political Economy of the World*

Trading System: From GATT to WTO (Oxford: Oxford University Press, 1995), Table 8.1, p. 208.

101 For a discussion of the MFA see Carl B. Hamilton (ed.), *Textiles Trade and Developing Countries: Eliminating the Multi-Fibre Arrangement in the 1990s* (Washington, DC: World Bank, 1990) and Vinod K. Aggarwal, *Liberal Protectionism: The International Politics of Organized Textile Protection*, (Berkeley, CA: University of California Press, 1985).

102 The exact impact of the MFA was difficult to calculate given the way in which importing signatories regarded it. See Carl B. Hamilton and Will Martin, 'Introduction', in Hamilton (ed.), *Textiles Trade and Developing Countries*, pp. 1–10. However, the general consensus is that it did stifle DC exports. For an analysis of the MFA's impact, see Refik Erzan, Junichi Goto and Paula Holmes, 'Effects of the Multi-Fibre Arrangement on Developing Countries' Trade: An Empirical Investigation', in Hamilton (ed.), *Textiles Trade and Developing Countries*, pp. 63–102.

103 See Henry R. Zheng, *Legal Structure of International Textile Trade* (New York: Quorum Books, 1988), p. 51.

104 See MFA, Article 11 (1), reproduced in the Appendix of this volume.

105 Ibid., Article 11 (5).

106 See Zheng, *Legal Structure of International Textile Trade*, p. 54.

107 This perspective was based on its understanding of the character of the GATT at the time. The EC insisted that the GATT was to resolve disputes through diplomacy instead of by adjudication. See Mora, 'A GATT with Teeth', p. 131.

108 See Aggarwal, *Liberal Protectionism*, p. 148.

109 Ibid., p. 149.

110 Idem.

111 Ibid., pp. 149–50.

112 See Zheng, *Legal Structure of International Textile Trade*, p. 54.

113 See MFA, Article 11 (8).

114 See Perlow, 'The Multilateral Supervision of International Trade', p. 109, n. 67.

115 See Beatrice Chaytor, 'Developing Countries and GATT/WTO Dispute Settlement: A Profile of Enforcement in Agriculture and Textiles', in Ernst-Ulrich Petersmann (ed.), *International Trade Law and the GATT/WTO Dispute Settlement System* (The Hague: Kluwer, 1997), pp. 347–55, at p. 351.

116 See *GATT BISD 27th Supplement*, pp. 119–26.

117 See Cline, *The Future of World Trade in Textiles and Apparel*, p. 171.

118 Ibid., p. 178. There are a number of reasons for this development. First, there was the backlog of quotas that had been unused as a result of the recession of 1980 and 1982. This provided for a sharp increase once demand had recovered. Second, there was the flexibility in the administration of quotas that permits importers both to 'swing' some portion of an underused quota to a product category where the quota is binding, and to shift quotas between years. Third, there may have been panic buying by importers in 1984 in anticipation of new import restrictions. Fourth, imports could have surged in uncontrollable products from uncontrollable suppliers. Ibid., p. 179. Other probabilities were the overvaluation of the dollar in 1984–85 and the fear in the US that the veto override on the Textile and Apparel Trade Enforcement Bill would again prove temporary. Ibid., p. 180.

119 See Vincent Cable, 'Textiles and Clothing', in J. Michael Finger and Andrzej Olechowski (eds), *The Uruguay Round: A Handbook on the Multilateral Trade Negotiations* (Washington, DC: World Bank, 1987), pp. 180–90, at p. 181.

120 See Ricardo Faini, Jaime de Melo and Wendy Takacs, *A Primer on the MFA Maze*, World Bank Policy Research Working Paper No. 1088 (Washington, DC: World Bank, 1993), p. 6.

121 See Jon G. Filipek, 'Agriculture in a World of Comparative Advantage: The Prospects for Farm Trade Liberalization in the Uruguay Round of GATT Negotiations', *Harvard International Law Journal*, Vol. 30, No. 1, 1989, pp. 123–70.

122 See Programme of Action Directed Towards an Expansion of International Trade, Decision of 17 November 1958, *GATT BISD 7th Supplement*, pp. 27–9.

123 Idem.

124 For instance, the FAO's Assistant Director-General has noted that until agricultural protection and support have been substantially reduced in developed countries, developing countries should not be required to further reduce bound tariffs or domestic subsidies. See FAO, 'Digesting Doha', *http://www.fao.org/news/2001/011106-e.htm.*

125 See First Report of Committee II, *GATT BISD 8th Supplement*, pp. 122–3.

126 Idem.

127 See *Reforming World Agricultural Trade: A Policy Statement by Twenty-nine Professionals from Seventeen Countries* (Washington, DC: Institute for International Economics/ Ottawa: Institute for Research on Public Policy, 1988), p. 22.

128 See John Charles Nagle, *Agricultural Trade Policies* (Farnborough: Saxon House, 1976), p. 89.

129 See Filipek, 'Agriculture in a World of Comparative Advantage', pp. 130–5; and Christopher Rusek, 'Trade Liberalization in Developed Countries: Movement Toward Market Control of Agricultural Trade in the United States, Japan and the European Union', *Administrative Law Review*, Vol. 48, No. 2, 1996, pp. 493–513.

130 See *GATT BISD 15th Supplement*, pp. 73–4.

131 Ibid., p. 74.

132 See Ministerial Declaration, 29 November 1982 in *GATT BISD 29th Supplement*, pp. 9–22.

133 Ibid., p. 17.

134 See Hudec, *Enforcing International Trade Law.*

135 Ibid., p. 327, Table 11.28.

136 Ibid., p. 333, Table 11.32.

137 Ibid., p. 334, Table 11.34.

138 Ibid., p. 335, Table 11.35.

139 Idem.

140 Ibid., p. 328.

141 See Protocol Amending the General Agreement on Tariffs and Trade to Introduce a Part IV on Trade and Development, 1965, *GATT BISD 13th Supplement*, pp. 2–9.

142 Ibid., pp. 75–6.

CHAPTER 3

1 See·Hudec, *Enforcing International Trade Law*, p. 120.

2 Ibid., pp. 122–3.

3 The developed countries had resisted the call for LDC observer status in the committees in 1979 on the grounds of efficiency and confidentiality of committee procedures. See Gilbert R. Winham, *International Trade and the Tokyo Round Negotiations* (Princeton, NJ: University of Princeton Press, 1986), p. 355.

4 See D.G. Beane, *The United States and the GATT: A Relational Study* (Amsterdam: Pergamon Press, 2000), and Ernest H Preeg, 'The US Leadership Role in World Trade: Past, Present, and Future', *Washington Quarterly*, Vol. 15, No. 2, 1992, pp. 81–91.

5 See Charles P. Kindleberger, *The World in Depression, 1929-1939* (Berkeley, CA: University of California Press, 1973); Stephen Krasner, 'State Power and the Structure of International Trade', *World Politics*, Vol. 28, No. 3, April 1976, pp. 317–47; Robert Keohane, 'The Theory of Hegemonic Stability and Changes in International Economic Regimes, 1967–1977', in Ole R. Holsti, Randolph M. Siverson and Alexander L. George (eds), *Change in the International System* (Boulder, CO: Westview Press, 1980); and Robert Gilpin, *The Political Economy of International Relations* (Princeton, NJ: Princeton University Press, 1987), pp. 75–80.

6 See Yarbrough and Yarbrough, 'Institutions for the Governance of Opportunism in International Trade', p. 133.

7 See Krueger, *Trade Policies and Developing Nations* (Washington, DC: Brookings Institution, 1995), p. 7.

8 Ibid., pp. 7–11. Whether import substitution was ever in favour in DCs generally has been challenged. See André Gunder Frank, *Dependent Accumulation and Under-Development* (London: Macmillan, 1978), pp. 128–30.

9 A number of explanations have been put forward for the failure of import substitution to benefit the DCs. See Henry J. Bruton, 'A Reconsideration of Import Substitution', *Journal of Economic Literature*, Vol. 36, June 1998, pp. 903–36.

10 See John Williamson, 'What Should the World Bank Think about the Washington Consensus?', *World Bank Research Observer*, Vol. 15, No. 2, 2000, pp. 251–64, at p. 251.

11 Ibid, p. 254.

12 Idem.

13 Ibid, p. 252. The full range was: fiscal discipline; a redirection of public expenditure towards primary health care, primary education and general infrastructure; tax reforms with the aim of broadening the tax base and lowering marginal rates of taxation; the liberalization of interest rates; competitive exchange rates; trade liberalization; the liberalization of national foreign direct investment regimes; the privatization of state-owned enterprises; deregulation, so as to encourage entry and exit of firms in and out of markets; and a secure legal framework for property rights. Ibid., pp. 252–3. For further analysis of the Washington Consensus, see Pedro-Pablo Kuczynski and John Williamson (eds), *After the Washington Consensus: Restarting Growth and Reform in Latin America* (Washington, DC: Institute for International Economics, 2003); Marcus Noland, *Reconsidering the Washington Consensus: The Lessons from Asian Industrial Policy* (Washington, DC: International Institute for Development Economics, 2002); and Joseph E. Stiglitz, *More Instruments and Broader Goals: Moving Toward the Post-Washington Consensus* (Helsinki: World Institute for Development Economics Research, United Nations University, 1998).

14 See Shahid Javed Burki and Guillermo Perry, *Beyond the Washington Consensus: Institutions Matter* (Washington, DC: World Bank, 1998).

15 See Ernest H. Preeg, *Traders in a Brave New World: The Uruguay Round and the Future of the International Trading System* (Chicago, IL: University of Chicago Press, 1995), p. 106.

16 Whether UNCTAD was ever a really effective organization for the articulation of DC demands is a moot point. See Robert Ramsey, 'UNCTAD's Failures: The Rich Get Richer', *International Organization*, Vol. 38, No. 2, 1984, pp. 387–97.

17 See Preeg, *Traders in a Brave New World*, p. 48.

18 It is possible that this realignment was the final stage of a process that began in the early 1960s. Diana Tussie suggests that in 1961 the active DCs were insisting on the reform of the GATT's rules on tariffs so as to exclude the DCs from the principle of reciprocity. However, by 1963 some DCs had adopted a 'less radical line' and were arguing for the GATT to adopt a range of measures that would result in lower barriers to the exports of the DCs. In effect there should be a fuller implementation of GATT rules and principles as regards their own particular exports. These diverse moves were a reflection of the dissimilarity of the DCs' circumstances. See Diane Tussie, *The Less Developed Countries and the World Trading System* (London: Pinter, 1987), pp. 27–8.

19 The Cairns Group was established in 1986. Its aim was to ensure that agricultural issues were given due consideration in the Uruguay Round. At the time of writing, its members are Argentina, Australia, Bolivia, Brazil, Canada, Chile, Colombia, Costa Rica, Guatemala, Indonesia, Malaysia, New Zealand, Paraguay, the Philippines, South Africa, Thailand and Uruguay. To date it has held 24 ministerial meetings on matters relating to international trade in agricultural products. Recent proposals submitted by it to the WTO CAG have concerned export restrictions, market access, domestic support and export competition. See, respectively, Cairns Group Negotiating Proposal on Export Restrictions (G/AG/NG/W93, 21 December 2000); Cairns Group Negotiating Proposal on Export Restrictions and Taxes (G/AG/NG/W/54, 10 November 2000); Cairns Group Negotiating Proposal on Domestic Support (G/AG/NG/W/35, 22 September 2000); and Cairns Group Negotiating Proposal on Export Competition (G/AG/NG/W/11, 16 June 2000). See <*http://www.cairnsgroup.org*>. For an analysis of its role, see Richard A. Higgott and Andrew Fenton Cooper, 'Middle Power Leadership and Coalition Building: Australia, the Cairns Group and the Uruguay Round of Trade Negotiations', *International Organization*, Vol. 44, No. 4, 1990, pp. 589–632.

20 See Preeg, *Traders in a Brave New World*, p. 59.

21 See Rajiv Kumar, 'Developing-Country Coalitions in International Trade Negotiations', in Diane Tussie and David Glover (eds), *The Developing Countries in World Trade: Policies and Bargaining Strategies* (Boulder, CO: Lynne Rienner, 1993), pp. 205–21, at p. 206.

22 Idem.

23 Idem. The G-77 was established in 1964 by 77 developing countries at the end of the first session of UNCTAD. From being mere signatories to the 'Joint Declaration of the Seventy-Seven Countries' the G-77 has developed an institutional structure. This has been done through the adoption of the Charter of Algiers in 1967, the creation of chapters in Rome, Vienna, Paris and Nairobi, and the establishment of the Group of 24 in Washington, DC. The Ministerial Meeting is the highest decision-making body of the G-77. These meetings are convened annually at the beginning of UN General Assembly meetings. They also occur periodically and in preparation for meetings of UNCTAD, the UN Industrial Development Organization and the UN Education, Scientific and Cultural Organization. See *www.g77.org*.

24 See Mary E. Footer, 'The Role of Consensus in GATT/WTO Decision-Making', *Northwestern Journal of International Law & Business*, Vol. 17, Nos 2 and 3, 1996–7, pp. 653–80.

25 See Kumar, 'Developing-Country Coalitions in International Trade Negotiations', p.206.

26 Ibid., p. 207.

27 This was pointed out to me during my interviews at the WTO, 20–21 April 2001.

28 See, for instance, Claude E. Barfield, *Free Trade, Sovereignty, Democracy: The Future of the World Trade Organization* (Washington, DC: American Enterprise Institute Press, 2001).

29 See Jesse Helms, 'American Sovereignty and the UN', *The National Interest*, Vol. 62, Winter, 2000–01, pp. 31–4.

30 Ibid., p. 34.

31 See Mora, 'A GATT with Teeth'.

32 See generally Lori Wallach and Michelle Sforza, *Whose Trade Organization? Corporate Globalization and the Erosion of Democracy: An Assessment of the World Trade Organization* (Washington, DC: Public Citizen, 1999).

33 Jeffrey Atik, 'Democratizing the WTO', *George Washington International Law Review*, Vol. 33, 2001, pp. 451–72.

34 Peter L. Lindseth, 'Democratic Legitimacy and the Administrative Character of Supranationalism: The Example of the European Community', *Columbia Law Review*, Vol. 99, No. 3, 1999, pp. 628–738.

35 See Sarah Dillon, 'Fuji Kodak, the WTO and the Death of Political Constituencies', *Minnesota Journal of Global Trade*, Vol. 8, No. 2, 1999, pp. 197–248. See 'EC – Regime for the Importation, Sale and Distribution of Bananas' (available at *www.wto.org*).

36 Ibid., p. 365.

CHAPTER 4

1 Agreement on Implementation of Article VI of the General Agreement on Tariffs and Trade 1994 (hereinafter the WTO Antidumping Code), in *The Results of the Uruguay Round*, pp. 147–71.

2 For a discussion of the WTO Antidumping Agreement, see David Palmeter, 'A Commentary on the WTO Anti-Dumping Code', *Journal of World Trade* Vol. 30, No. 4, 1996, pp. 43–69; Raj Krishna, *Antidumping in Law and Practice*, World Bank Policy Research Working Paper No. 1823 (Washington, DC: World Bank, 1997); and Gary N. Horlick and Eleanor C. Shea, 'The World Trade Organization Anti-dumping Agreement', *Journal of World Trade*, Vol. 29, No. 1, 1995, pp. 5–31. For issues relating to the DCs, see Inge Nora Neufeld, *Anti-Dumping and Countervailing Procedures: Use or Abuse? Implications for Developing Countries* (New York: UNCTAD, 2001), and J. Luis Guasch and Sarath Rajapatirana, *Antidumping and Competition Policies in Latin America and the Caribbean: Total Strangers or Soul Mates?*, World Bank Policy Research Working Paper No. 1958 (Washington, DC: World Bank, 1998).

3 See the WTO Antidumping Agreement, Article 16 (1). (Article 16 of the 1995 Anti-dumping Code, which establishes the CADP, is in the Appendix to this volume.)

4 One major outcome of the Uruguay Round was that it was a single undertaking whereby all the WTO's members became party to all the multilateral trade agreements.

5 See DSU, Article 1 and Appendix 1. For our purposes here, we should note that the TMB still has a dispute settlement role.

6 See Mora, 'A GATT with Teeth', p. 142.

7 See G/ADD/9, Committee on Anti-Dumping Practices, Minutes of the Regular Meeting (21–22 October 1996), *http://www.wto.org/search97cgi/s97_cgi*, para. 98. Only the delegate of Malaysia purported to speak up expressly on behalf of a group of DCs.

Ibid., para. 108. See also comments by Singapore and Malaysia, as the only instances of real LDC cooperation, in Committee on Anti-Dumping Practices, Minutes of the Regular Meeting (28–29 April 1997) paras 93–8 and 112 respectively.

8   Interviews at the WTO in Geneva, 20–21 April 2001.

9   Interviews at the WTO in Geneva, 20–21 April 2001.

10 The Ad Hoc Committee is to meet at least twice a year, in conjunction with the regular meetings of the CADP in order to facilitate participation by experts from national capitals. Additional meetings can be scheduled if the members participating conclude that such additional meetings would be useful. See 'Summary Report of the Meeting of the Ad Hoc Group on Implementation of the Committee on Anti-dumping Practices', Note by the Secretariat, G/ADP/AHG/R/1, 22 October 1996, *http://www.wto.org/search97cgi/s97_cgi*, p. 5, para. 5 (visited on 11 January 2001). The page numbers here are based on the copy obtained from this website.

11 See Kufuor, *The Growing Problem of Intra-LDC Antidumping Actions in World Trade.*

12 See Summary Report of the Meeting of the Ad Hoc Group on Implementation of the Committee on Anti-Dumping Practices, 29–30 April 1997, G/ADP/AHG/R/2, Note by the Secretariat, *http://www.wto.org/search97cgi/s97*, paras 3–9 (visited on 11 January 2001).

13 Report of the Committee on Antidumping Practices (October 2002), p. 5, note 2.

14 Ibid., p. 3.

15 Only India, Turkey, Brazil and Indonesia have submitted proposals to it. Ibid., p. 4.

16 See Stewart, *The GATT Uruguay Round*, p. 1616.

17 Idem.

18 Idem.

19 Ibid., p. 1624.

20 However, see, Decision on Anti-Circumvention in *The Results of the Uruguay Round*, p. 397.

21 For a general introduction to anti-circumvention law and the practice of the WTO's members see, for example, Simon Holmes, 'Anti-circumvention under the European Union's New Anti-Dumping Rules', *Journal of World Trade*, Vol. 29, No. 3, 1995, pp. 161–80, and Rainer M. Bierwagen, *GATT Article VI and the Protectionist Bias in Anti-Dumping Laws* (Deventer, The Netherlands: Kluwer Law and Taxation, 1990), pp. 34–7.

22 On problems of technical assistance on GATT/WTO matters for the DCs, see Mary E. Footer, 'Technical Assistance and Trade Law Reform Post-Doha: Brave New World', in John Hatchard and Amanda Perry-Kessaris (eds), *Law and Development: Facing Complexity in the 21st Century* (London: Cavendish, 2003), pp. 108–31.

23 Report of the Committee on Antidumping Practices (2002), p. 14.

24 Ibid., pp. 12–13.

25 See the Preamble of the ATC.

26 For an analysis of the ATC, see Maarten Smeets, 'Main Features of the Uruguay Round Agreement on Textiles and Clothing, and Implications for the Trading System', *Journal of World Trade*, Vol. 29, No. 5, 1995, pp. 97–108; Kim Fae Sung, Kenneth A. Reinert and Chris G. Rodrigo, 'The Agreement on Textiles and Clothing: Safeguard Actions from 1995–2001', *Journal of International Economic Law*, Vol. 5, No. 2, 2002, pp. 445–68.

27 See ATC, Article 2.

28 Ibid., Article 6.

29 Ibid. Article 8 (1). (See the Appendix for Article 8 of the ATC.)

30 Idem.

31 Ibid., Article 2 (1).

32 See Agency for International Trade Information and Cooperation, 'Textiles and Clothing: Implications for Less-Advantaged Developing Countries', http://www. acici.org/aitic/documents/Reports/report 2ang.html, p. 3. Also, the possibility of extending the ATC was pointed out to me by staff at the WTO during my interviews there on 20–21 April 2001.

33 See United States International Trade Commission, *Potential Impact on the U.S. Economy and Industries of the GATT Uruguay Round Agreements*, June 1994.

34 John M. Jennings, 'In Search of a Standard: "Serious Damage" in the Agreement on Textiles and Clothing', *Northwestern Journal of International Law and Business*, Vol. 17, No. 1, 1996, pp. 272–319, at p. 277.

35 See John H. Jackson, 'The Crumbling Institutions of the Liberal Trade System'.

36 See ATC, Article 6 (13).

37 Ibid., Article 8 (7).

38 Ibid., Article 6 (10).

39 See Steven P. Crowley and John H. Jackson, 'WTO Dispute Procedures, Standard of Review, and Deference to National Governments', *American Journal of International Law*, Vol. 90, No. 2, 1996, pp. 193–213, at pp. 194–5.

40 Ibid., Article 10.

41 See Jennings, 'In Search of a Standard', p. 303.

42 See USTR, *Annual Report March 2000* (Textiles Monitoring Body), p. 2.

43 Ibid., p. 3.

44 See Report of the Textiles Monitoring Body (20 October 2000).

45 Idem.

46 Idem.

47 For an introduction to the WTO Agreement on Agriculture, see Jeffrey J. Steinle, 'The Problem Child of World Trade: Reform School for Agriculture', *Minnesota Journal of Global Trade*, Vol. 4, No. 2, 1995, pp. 333–60. For the DC agricultural agenda in the Doha Round see Alan Matthews, 'Developing Country Positions in WTO Agricultural Trade Negotiations', *Development Policy Review*, Vol. 20, No. 1, 2002, pp. 75–90, and Merlinda D. Ingco (ed.), *Agriculture, Trade and the WTO: Creating a Trading Environment of Development*, World Bank Policy Research Working Paper No. 1271 (Washington, DC: World Bank, 2003).

48 See Preamble to Agreement on Agriculture, in *The Results of the Uruguay Round*, pp. 33–58.

49 Ibid., Articles 4 and 9.

50 Ibid., Article 17.

51 The Agreement leaves this to the Dispute Settlement Body. Ibid., Article 19.

52 See *Annual Report – World Trade Organization* (1995), p. 2. This report is downloaded from <http://www.ustr.gov/html/1996_tpa_wto_3.html>.

53 Idem.

54 This is officially called the Annual Monitoring Exercise in Respect of the Follow-Up to the Ministerial Decision on Measures Concerning the Possible Negative Effects of the Reform Programme on Least-Developed and Net Food-Importing Countries.

55 See FAO, *Technical Assistance and the Uruguay Round Agreements* (Rome: Food and Agriculture Organization of the United Nations, 2nd edn, 1998), pp. 9–10.

56 See *Annual Report – WTO*, p. 75.

57 This was pointed out to me during my discussions at the WTO, 20– 21 April 2001.

58 On the view that Special and Differential Treatment rules are legally binding and thus enforceable under the WTO, see Edwini Kessie, 'Enforceability of the Legal Provisions Relating to Special and Differential Treatment under the WTO Agreements', *Journal of World Intellectual Property*, Vol. 3, 2000, pp. 955–75, at p. 955.

59 See Committee on Agriculture (special session) G/AG/NG/W/142, (23 March 2001).

60 Ibid., paras 8 and 13.

61 See GATT Doc. G/L/131 Report by the Committee on Agriculture – Report adopted by the Committee on Agriculture on 6 November 1996, p. 3.

62 See GATT Doc. G/AG/NG/R/7, Committee on Agriculture, Special Session, 'Summary Report of Seventh Meeting of the Special Session', Note by the Secretariat, 26–27 March 2001, p. 2.

63 Ibid., pp. 3 and 5.

64 Ibid., pp. 7–8.

65 See ibid., p. 6.

66 See Agreement on Agriculture, Article 10 (2).

67 Ibid., Article 10 (1).

68 See 'Proposal by MERCOSUR to the Committee on Agriculture, WTO Negotiations on Agriculture – Export Credits for Agricultural Markets', G/AG/NG/W/139 (20 March 2001).

69 Idem.

70 See Market Access, Submission by Cuba, Dominican Republic, El Salvador, Honduras, Kenya, India, Nigeria, Pakistan, Sri Lanka, Uganda, and Zimbabwe (28 September 2000), pp. 3–4 for this and the following paragraphs.

71 See Agreement on Agriculture, Article 5 (1).

72 Idem.

73 See WTO, Agriculture negotiations: Backgrounder, *htpp://www.wto.org/wto/english/tratop_e/agric_e/ negs_bkgrnd07_access_e.htm* (visited on 22 July 2002).

74 Idem.

75 The Article 20 reform process sets out the members' decision to initiate reforms to the Agreement one year before the end of its implementation period.

76 See AIE/6: Paper by Pakistan, Peru, and the Dominican Republic on Issues of Interest to Developing Countries – 19 September 1997; AIE/8: Paper by Uruguay on Implementation of Tariff Commitments – 24 October 1997; and AIE/12: Paper by Cuba on Special and Differential Treatment and Food Importing Developing Countries – 18 December 1997.

77 AIE/30: Paper submitted by India – Issues of Interest to Developing Countries – 23 June 1998; AIE/31: Paper by Brazil – Trade Liberalization: Sectoral and 'Across the Board' Initiatives – 6 July 1998; AIE/32: Paper by Argentina – Non-Trade Concerns in the Next Agricultural Negotiations – 27 July 1998; AIE/33: Paper by South Africa – The Effect of Inflation on Reduction Commitments – 29 July 1998; AIE/39: Paper by the Republic of Korea – Non-Trade Concerns in Net Food-Importing Countries – 22 September 1998; AIE/41: Paper by South Africa – The Negative Effects of Export Subsidies on Developing Countries – 26 October 1998; AIE/43: Paper by Uruguay – Tariff Peaks and Tariff Escalation – 4 November 1998; AIE/44: Paper by India – Food Security – An Important Non-Trade Concern – 16 November 1998.

78 AIE/51: Paper by Mauritius – Multifunctional Role of Agriculture in Small Island Developing States – 10 March 1999; AIE/54: Paper by El Salvador, Honduras, Cuba,

Nicaragua, the Dominican Republic and Pakistan – Issues Related to Market Access – 23 March 1999; AIE/58: Paper by Uruguay – Agreed Conclusions of an UNCTAD Expert Meeting on Trade in Agriculture Held on 26 April 1999 – 7 June 1999; AIE/59: Paper by Malaysia, Myanmar, Philippines and Thailand – Continuation of the Reform Process after the End of the Implementation Period – 7 June 1999; AIE/63: Paper by Cuba, the Dominican Republic, El Salvador, Honduras, Nicaragua, Pakistan, Sri Lanka and Uganda – Agreement on Agriculture: Issues Related to Special and Differential Treatment – 22 June 1999; AIE/65: Paper by Mauritius – Agriculture in Small Island Developing States – 9 July 1999; AIE/70: Paper by El Salvador, Cuba, Honduras, the Dominican Republic, Pakistan, Sri Lanka and Zimbabwe – Agreement on Agriculture: Special and Differential Treatment – Non-Paper 2 – 24 September 1999; AIE/74: Paper by Uruguay – The Multifunctional Character of Agriculture and Land – 28 September 1999.

79 AIE/S6: Special and Differential Treatment Provisions Relating to the Agreement on Agriculture – 16 February 1998; AIE/S7: Studies on the Implementation and Impact of the Agreement on Agriculture on Developing Countries – 24 February 1998; AIE/S8/Rev.1: NFIDC Decision – Actions Taken Within the Framework of the Decision as Notified by Members – Revision 24 February 1999; AIE/S10/Rev.1: Agricultural Trade Performance by Developing Countries – Revision 17 February 1999; AIE/S13: Tariff Treatment of Products of Special Interest to Developing Country Members – 28 July 1999.

80 See Steve Charnovitz, 'The World Trade Organization and the Environment', *Yearbook of International Environmental Law*, Vol. 8, 1997, pp. 98–116. However, this did not mean that the GATT's drafters were not aware of the emerging concern about the impact of international trade on natural resources. Ibid., pp. 103–4. This was supposedly due to the lack of a well-organized environmental civil society in the US and Europe. See Schaffer, 'The World Trade Organization under Challenge', p. 17.

81 See Emerging Environmental Debate in GATT/WTO: EMIT – GATT Group on Environmental Measures in International Trade, *http://www.wto.org*.

82 See Schaffer, 'The World Trade Organization', p. 17.

83 Ibid., p. 18.

84 Ibid., p. 19.

85 See Decision on Trade and Environment, in *The Results of the Uruguay Round*, pp. 469–71.

86 Ibid., para. (a).

87 Ibid,, para. (b).

88 See Frank Bierman, 'The Rising Tide of Green Unilateralism in World Trade Law: Options for Reconciling the Emerging North–South Conflict', *Journal of World Trade*, Vol. 35, No. 3, 2001, pp. 421–48.

89 See Sabine Shaw and Risa Schwarz, 'Trade and Environment in the WTO: State of Play', *Journal of World Trade*, Vol. 36, No.1, 2002, pp. 129–54.

90 See CTE, 'Report of the Meeting Held on 24–25 July 1996'.

91 This is based on submissions made either individually or jointly by DCs or in circumstances in which DCs and developed countries make a joint submission with DCs making up at least half of the members involved in the submission.

92 See Beatrice Chaytor, 'Cooperation Between Governments and NGOs: The Case of Sierra Leone in the CTE', in Pieder Konz et al. (eds), *Trade, Environment and Sustainable Development: Views from Sub-Saharan Africa and Latin America – A Reader*

(Tokyo: United Nations University/Geneva: International Centre for Trade and Sustainable Development), pp. 89–93.

93 See Fiona Macmillan, *WTO and the Environment* (London: Sweet & Maxwell, 2001), p. 14.

94 Although decided on non-discrimination grounds, the following are the key panel reports with implications for trade and the environment, and they bear out the assertion that the panels favour trade over conservation: 'GATT Report of the Panel: United States – Restriction on Imports of Tuna', *GATT BISD 39th Supplement*, pp. 155–205; 'GATT Dispute Settlement Panel Report on United States Restrictions on Imports of Tuna', *International Legal Materials*, Vol. 33, 1994, pp. 839–902; 'WTO Report of the Panel: United States – Standards for Reformulated and Conventional Gasoline', *International Legal Materials*, Vol. 35, 1996, pp. 274–300; and 'WTO Report of the Appellate Body: United States – Standards for Reformulated Gasoline', *International Legal Materials*, Vol. 35, 1996, pp. 603–34.

95 See Schaffer, 'The World Trade Organization under Challenge', p. 46.

96 See Shaw and Schwartz, 'Trade and Environment in the WTO', p. 130.

97 See Schaffer, 'The World Trade Organization under Challenge', pp. 45–6.

98 See Jackson, 'The Crumbling Institutions of the Liberal Trading System'.

99 For a discussion of this complaint, see Cynthia M. Maas, 'Should the WTO Expand GATT Article XX: An Analysis of United States – Standards for Reformulated and Conventional Gasoline', *Minnesota Journal of Global Trade*, Vol. 5, No. 2, Summer 1996, pp. 415–39.

100 Here the panel found that the US regulations were clearly aimed at protecting life or health as required by GATT Article XX (b). However, it supported Brazil and Venezuela by ruling that the gasoline regulations were not necessary under Article XX, as in its view the US clearly had options other than the gasoline regulation, which discriminated against foreign imports.

101 For a discussion of the *Shrimp-Turtle* dispute, see Bret Puls, 'The Murky Waters of International Environmental Jurisprudence: A Critique of Recent WTO Holdings in the Shrimp/Turtle Controversy', *Minnesota Journal of Global Trade*, Vol. 8, No. 2, Summer 1999, pp. 343–79.

102 Concern about the high turtle death rate led the US to adopt turtle exclusion devices (TEDs) to enable trapped turtles escape from shrimp nets and avoid being killed in the process of shrimp fishing. In 1989 the US then enacted the Sea Turtle Conservation Amendments to the Endangered Species Act. This act established the regulations banning imports of shrimp and shrimp products harvested through commercial fishing methods that harmed sea turtles. Specifically, it targeted shrimp and shrimp products from countries that failed to receive certification by the US under the regulations. The amendments required the US Secretary of State both to initiate negotiations with all foreign countries in order to develop treaties protecting sea turtles and to report on those negotiations to Congress. The amendments also required the secretaries of State, Commerce and Treasury to prohibit shrimp products from entering the US if the exporting country failed to mandate the use of shrimp nets equipped with TEDs.

103 See Shaw and Schwartz, 'Trade and the Environment', p. 147.

104 Idem.

105 See Preamble to Agreement Establishing the World Trade Organization, in *Results of the Uruguay Round*.

106 Agreement on the Application of Sanitary and Phytosanitary Measures, in *Results of the Uruguay Round*, pp. 69–85.

107 See Preamble to Agreement on Agriculture.

108 See Agreement on the Application of Sanitary and Phytosanitary Measures.

109 See Shaw and Schwarz, 'Trade and the Environment in the WTO', p. 149.

110 Idem.

111 For an overall analysis of this see Padideh Ala'i, 'Free Trade or Sustainable Development? An Analysis of the WTO Appellate Body's Shift to a More Balanced Approach to Trade Liberalization', *American University International Law Review*, Vol. 14, No. 4, 1999, pp. 1129–71.

112 Ibid., p. 1130.

113 Ibid., pp. 1130–1.

114 The SPS Agreement establishes the Committee on Sanitary and Phytosanitary Measures under Article 12. See SPS Agreement. Under Article 12(4) of the agreement, the SPS Committee is placed under an obligation to 'establish a list of international guidelines or recommendations relating to sanitary or phytosanitary measures which the Committee determines to have a major trade impact'. Idem.

115 See Shaw and Schwarz, 'Trade and the Environment in the WTO'.

116 See *1996 CTE Report*, p. 2.

117 Idem.

118 See Jose Maria Figueres Olsen et al., 'Trade and Environment at the World Trade Organization: The Need for a Constructive Dialogue', in Gary Sampson (ed.), *The Role of the World Trade Organization in Global Governance* (Tokyo: United Nations University Press, 2001), pp. 155–82.

119 See *1996 CTE Report*, p. 2.

120 Ibid., pp. 2–3.

121 Ibid., p. 3.

122 For an introduction to eco-labelling and international trade, see Surya P. Subedi, 'Balancing International Trade with Environmental Protection: International Legal Aspects of Eco-Labels', *Brooklyn Journal of International Law*, Vol. 25, No. 2, 1999; pp. 373–405; Christian Tietje, 'Voluntary Eco-Labelling Programmes and Questions of State Responsibility in the WTO/GATT Legal System', *Journal of World Trade*, Vol. 29, No. 5, 1995, pp. 123–58, and Elliot B. Staffin, 'Trade Barrier or Trade Boon? A Critical Evaluation of Environmental Labelling and its Role in the "Greening" of World Trade', *Columbia Journal of Environmental Law*, Vol. 21, No. 2, 1996, p. 205.

123 See *1996 CTE Report*, p. 12.

124 Ibid., p. 37.

CHAPTER 5

1 See Richard Blackhurst et al., 'Options for Improving Africa's Participation in the WTO', *The World Economy*, Vol. 23, No. 4, 2000, pp. 491–510, at p. 492.

2 On the importance of links between trade representatives in Geneva and national trade officials, see Chaytor, 'Cooperation Between Governments and NGOs'. However, delegations may find it hard to be flexible when carrying out negotiations. See Sheila Page, *Developing Countries in GATT/WTO Negotiations* (London: Overseas Development Institute, 2001), p. 2.

3   See Constantine Michalopolous, *Developing Country Participation in the WTO*, World Bank Policy Research Working Paper No. 1906 (Washington, DC: World Bank), pp. 19–20.

4   Ibid., p. 20.

5   For a discussion of principal–agent issues, see David E.M. Sapington, 'Incentives in Principal–Agent Relationships', *Journal of Economic Perspectives*, Vol. 5, No. 2, 1991, pp. 45–66.

6   See Oxfam GB, *Institutional Reform of the WTO*, March 2000, p. 11.

7   Ibid. p. 12.

8   Idem.

9   See Page, *Developing Countries in GATT/WTO Negotiations*, p. 35.

10 See Jackson, *The World Trade Organization: Constitution and Jurisprudence*, pp. 53–4.

11 Jorge B. Riaboi, 'Trade Liberalization and Dangerous Political Games', *Fordham International Law Journal*, Vol. 24, Nos 1 and 2, 2000, pp. 572–607, pp. 572, 574.

12 See Todd Zywicki, *Baptists: The Political Economy of Political Environmental Interest Groups*, George Mason University Law and Economics Working Paper No. 23 (Arlington, VA: George Mason University, 2002).

13 Rubens Ricupero, 'Rebuilding Confidence in the Multilateral Trading System: Closing the Legitimacy Gap', in Gary P. Sampson (ed.), *The Role of the World Trade Organization in Global Governance* (Tokyo: United Nations University, 2001), pp. 37–58, at p. 49.

Bibliography

BOOKS AND ARTICLES

Abbott, Frederick M., 'Distributed Governance at the WTO-WIPO: An Evolving Model for Open-Architecture Integrated Governance', in Marco Bronckers and Reinhard Quick (eds), *New Directions in International Economic Law: Essays in Honour of John H. Jackson* (The Hague: Kluwer Law International, 2000), pp. 15–33.

Abbott, Kenneth W., 'The Trading Nation's Dilemma: The Functions of the Law of International Trade', *Harvard Journal of International Law*, Vol. 26, No. 2, 1985, pp. 501–32.

Abbott, Kenneth W., and Duncan Snidal, 'Hard and Soft Law in International Governance', *International Organization*, Vol. 54, 2000, pp. 421–56.

Aceves, William J., 'Lost Sovereignty? The Implications of the Uruguay Round Agreements', *Fordham Journal of International Law*, Vol. 19, 1995, pp. 427–74.

Adamantopolous, Konstantin, and Diego De Notaris, 'The Future of the WTO and the Reform of the Anti-Dumping Agreement: A Legal Perspective', *Fordham Journal of International Law*, Vol. 24, 2000, pp. 30–61.

Aggarwal, Vinod K., *Liberal Protectionism: The International Politics of Organized Textile Trade* (Berkeley, CA: University of California Press, 1985).

El-Agraa, Ali, 'VERs as a Prominent Feature of Japanese Trade Policy: Their Rationale, Costs and Benefits', *World Economy*, Vol. 18, 1995, pp. 219–35.

Ahn, Dukgeun, 'Linkages between International Financial and Trade Institutions – IMF, World Bank and WTO', *Journal of World Trade*, Vol. 34, 2000, pp. 1–35.

Akakwam, Philip, 'The Standard of Review in the 1994 Antidumping Code: Circumscribing the Role of GATT Panels in Reviewing National Antidumping Determinations', *Minnesota Journal of Global Trade*, Vol. 5, 1996, pp. 277–310.

Ala'i, Padideh, 'Free Trade or Sustainable Development? An Analysis of the WTO Appellate Body's Shift to a More Balanced Approach to Trade Liberalization', *American University International Law Review*, Vol. 14, No. 4, 1999, pp. 1129–71.

Amorim, Celso L.N., 'The WTO from the Perspective of a Developing Country', *Fordham Journal of International Law*, Vol. 24, 2000, pp. 95–106.

Anell, Lars, and Brigitta Nygren, *The Developing Countries and the World Economic Order* (London: Pinter, 1980).

Arrow, Kenneth J., *Social Choice and Individual Values* (New York: Wiley, 2nd edn, 1963).

Atik, Jeffrey, 'Democratizing the WTO', *George Washington Law Review*, Vol. 33, 2001, pp. 451–72.

Awuku, Emmanuel Opoku, 'How Do the Results of the Uruguay Round Affect the North–South Trade?', *Journal of World Trade*, Vol. 28, 1994, pp. 75–93.

Axelrod, Robert, *The Evolution of Cooperation* (New York: Basic Books, 1984).

Bacchus, James, 'Groping Toward Grotius: The WTO and the International Rule of Law', *Harvard Journal of International Law*, Vol. 44, No. 2, 2003, pp. 533–50.

Barfield, Claude E., *Free Trade, Sovereignty, Democracy: The Future of the World Trade Organization* (Washington, DC: American Enterprise Institute Press, 2001).

Beane, D.G., *The United States and the GATT: A Relational Study* (Amsterdam: Pergamon Press, 2000).

Bhagwati, Jagdish, *Protectionism* (Cambridge, MA: MIT Press, 1988).

Bhala, Raj, 'The Banana War', *McGeorge Law Review*, Vol. 31, 2000, pp. 839–971.

Bhala, Raj, 'Marxist Origins of the "Anti-Third World" Claim', *Fordham Journal of International Law*, Vol. 24, 2000, pp. 132–57.

Bierman, Frank, 'The Rising Tide of Green Unilateralism in World Trade Law: Options for Reconciling the Emerging North–South Conflict', *Journal of World Trade*, Vol. 35, No. 3, 2001, pp. 421–48.

Bierwagen, Rainer, *GATT Article VI and the Protectionist Bias in Anti-Dumping Laws* (Deventer, The Netherlands: Kluwer Law and Taxation, 1990).

Blackhurst, Richard, Bill Lyakurwa and Ademola Oyejide, 'Options for Improving Africa's Participation in the WTO', *The World Economy*, Vol. 23, 2000, pp. 491–510.

Blokker, Niels, *International Regulation of World Trade in Textiles: Lessons for Practice: A Contribution to Theory* (Dordrecht, The Netherlands: Martinus Nijhoff, 1989).

Bronckers, Marco C.J., 'More Power to the WTO?', *Journal of International Economic Law*, Vol. 4, 2000, pp. 41–65.

Bruton, Henry J., 'A Reconsideration of Import Substitution', *Journal of Economic Literature*, Vol. 36, June 1998, pp. 903–36.

Buchanan, James M. and Gordon Tullock, *The Calculus of Consent: Logical Foundations of Constitutional Democracy* (Ann Arbor, MI: University of Michigan Press, 1962).

Bull, Hedley, *The Anarchical Society: A Study of World Order in Politics* (New York: Columbia University Press, 2nd edn, 1977).

Burki, Shahid Javed, and Guillermo Perry, *Beyond the Washington Consensus: Institutions Matter* (Washington, DC: World Bank, 1998).

Burley, Anne-Marie Slaughter, 'International Law and International Relations Theory: A Dual Agenda', *American Journal of International Law*, Vol. 87, No. 2, 1993, pp. 205–39.

Cable, Vincent, 'Textiles and Clothing', in J. Michael Finger and Andrezj Olechowski (eds), *The Uruguay Round: A Handbook of Multilateral Trade Negotiations* (Washington, DC: World Bank, 1987), pp. 180–90.

Carr, E.H., *The Twenty Years' Crisis, 1919–1939: An Introduction to the Study of International Relations* (London and New York: Torchbooks, 1964.

Charnovitz, Steve, 'The World Trade Organization and the Environment', *Yearbook of International Environmental Law*, Vol. 8, 1997, pp. 98–116.

Chaytor, Beatrice, 'Cooperation Between Governments and NGOs: The Case of Sierra Leone in the CTE', in Pieder Konz, Christophe Bellman, Lucas Assuncao and Ricardo Melendez-Oritz (eds), *Trade, Environment and Sustainable Development: Views from Sub-Saharan Africa and Latin America – A Reader* (Tokyo: United Nations University/Geneva: The International Centre for Trade and Sustainable Development, 2000), pp. 89–93.

Chaytor, Beatrice, 'Developing Countries and GATT/WTO Dispute Settlement: A Profile of Enforcement in Agriculture and Textiles', in Ernst-Ulrich Petersmann (ed.), *International Trade Law and the GATT/WTO Dispute Settlement System* (The Hague: Kluwer, 1997), pp. 347–55.

Chaytor, Beatrice, and Mathias Wolkewitz, 'Participation and Priorities: An Assessment of Developing Country Concerns in the Trade/Environment Interface', *Review of European Community and International Environmental Law*, Vol. 6, July 1997, pp. 157–62.

Checkel, Jeffrey T., *Why Comply? Constructivism, Social Norms and the Study of International Institutions*, Arena Working Paper 99/24, *http://www.arena.uio.no/publications/wp99_24.htm*.

Cline, William R., *The Future of World Trade in Textiles and Apparel* (Washington, DC: Institute for International Economics, 1987).

Coase, Ronald, 'The Problem of Social Cost', *Journal of Law and Economics*, Vol. 3, No. 1, 1960, pp. 1–44.

Coase, Ronald, 'The Nature of the Firm', *Economica*, Vol. 4, 1937, pp. 386–405.

Croome, John, *Reshaping the World Trading System: A History of the Uruguay Round* (The Hague: Kluwer Law International, 1999).

Crowley, Steven P., and John H. Jackson, 'WTO Dispute Procedures, Standard of Review, and Deference to National Governments', *American Journal of International Law*, Vol. 90, No. 2, 1996, pp. 193–213.

Demaret, Paul, 'The Metamorphoses of the GATT: From the Havana Charter to the World Trade Organization', *Columbia Journal of Transnational Law*, Vol. 34, No. 1, 1995, pp. 123–71.

Desta, Melaku Geboye, *The Law of International Trade in Agricultural Products from GATT 1947 to WTO Agreement on Agriculture* (The Hague: Kluwer Law International, 2002).

Desta, Melaku Geboye, 'Food Security and International Trade Law: An Appraisal of the World Trade Organization Approach', *Journal of World Trade*, Vol. 35, 2001, pp. 449–68.

Dillon, Sarah, 'Fuji Kodak, the WTO and the Death of Political Constituencies', *Minnesota Journal of Global Trade*, Vol. 8, No. 2, 1999, pp. 197–248.

Dunn, K. Kristine, 'The Textiles Monitoring Body: Can it Bring Textiles Trade into GATT?', *Minnesota Journal of Global Trade*, Vol. 7, No. 1, 1998, pp. 123–5.

Dutz, Mark A., *Enforcement of Canadian 'Unfair' Trade Laws: The Case for Competition Policies as an Antidote for Protection*, World Bank Policy Research Working Paper No. 776 (Washington, DC: World Bank, 1991).

Dymond, William and Michael M. Hart, 'Post-Modern Trade Policy – Reflections on the Challenges to Multilateral Trade Negotiations after Seattle', *Journal of World Trade*, Vol. 34, 2000, pp. 2–38.

Eglin, Richard, 'Surveillance of Balance-of-Payments Measures in the GATT', *The World Economy*, Vol. 10, No. 1, 1987, pp. 1–26.

Ellikson, Robert C., 'A Hypothesis of Wealth-Maximizing Norms: Evidence from the Whaling Industry', *Journal of Law, Economics and Organization*, Vol. 5, No. 1, 1989, pp. 83–97.

Erzan, Refik, Junichi Goto and Paula Holmes, 'Effects of the Multi-Fibre Arrangement on Developing Countries Trade: An Empirical Investigation', in Carl B. Hamilton (ed.), *Textiles Trade and Developing Countries: Eliminating the Multi-Fibre Arrangement in the 1990s* (Washington, DC: World Bank, 1990), pp. 63–102.

Evans, Edward E., and Carlton G. Davis, 'United States Sugar and Sweeteners Markets: Implications for CARICOM Tariff-Rate Quota Holders', *Social and Economic Studies*, Vol. 49, 2000, pp. 1–36.

Evans, Gail E., *Lawmaking under the Trade Constitution: A Study in Legislating by the World Trade Organization*, Studies in Transnational Economic Law (The Hague/ Boston: Kluwer Law International, 2000).

Eymann, Angelika, and Ludger Schuknecht, *Antidumping Enforcement in the European Community*, World Bank Policy Research Working Paper No. 743 (Washington, DC: World Bank, 1991).

Faini, Ricardo, Jaime de Melo and Wendy Takacs, *A Primer on the MFA Maze*, World Bank Policy Research Working Paper No. 1088 (Washington, DC: World Bank, 1993).

Filipek, Jon G., 'Agriculture in a World of Comparative Advantage: The Prospects for Farm Trade Liberalization in the Uruguay Round of GATT Negotiations', *Harvard International Law Journal*, Vol. 30, No. 1, 1989, pp. 123–70.

Finger, J. Michael, *The Meaning of 'Unfair' in U.S. Import Policy*, World Bank Policy Research Working Paper No. 745 (Washington, DC: World Bank, 1991).

Finger, J. Michael, *The Origins and Evolution of Antidumping Regulation*, World Bank Policy Research Working Paper No. 783 (Washington, DC: World Bank, 1991).

Finger, J. Michael, and L. Alan Winters, 'What can the WTO Do for Developing Countries?', in Anne O. Krueger (ed.), *The WTO as an International Organization* (Chicago: University of Chicago Press, 1998), pp. 365–92.

Finger, J. Michael, and Sumana Dhar, *Do Rules Control Power? GATT Articles and Arrangements in the Uruguay Round*, World Bank Policy Research Working Paper No. 818 (Washington, DC: World Bank, 1992).

Footer, Mary E., 'Technical Assistance and Trade Law Reform Post-Doha: Brave New World', in John Hatchard and Amanda Perry-Kessaris (eds), *Law and Development: Facing Complexity in the 21st Century* (London: Cavendish, 2003), pp. 108–31.

Footer, Mary E., 'The Role of Consensus in GATT/WTO Decision-Making', *Northwestern University Journal of International Law & Business*, Vol. 17, Nos 2 and 3, 1996–7, pp. 653–80.

Frank, André G., *Dependent Accumulation and Under-Development* (London: Macmillan, 1978).

s

Gaines, Sanford, 'The WTO's Reading of the GATT Article XX Chapeau: A Disguised Restriction on Environmental Measures', *University of Pennsylvania Journal of International Economic Law*, Vol. 22, 2001, pp. 739–863.

Gallagher, Peter, *Guide to the WTO and Developing Countries* (The Hague: Kluwer Law International, 2000).

Gerhart, Peter M., 'The Two Constitutional Visions of the World Trade Organization', *University of Pennsylvania Journal of International Economic Law*, Vol. 24, No. 5, 2003, pp. 1–75.

Gerhart, Peter M., 'Reflections on the WTO Doha Ministerial: Slow Transformations: The WTO as a Distributive Organization', *American University International Law Review*, Vol. 17, No. 5, 2002, pp. 1045–95.

Gibson, Paul, John Vainio, Dan Whitley and Mary Bohman, *Profiles of Tariffs in Global Agricultural Markets* (Washington, DC: United States Department of Agriculture, 2001).

Gilpin, Robert, *The Political Economy of International Relations* (Princeton, NJ: Princeton University Press, 1987).

Gilpin, Robert, *U.S. Power and the Multinational Corporation: The Political Economy of Foreign Direct Investment* (New York: Basic Books, 1975).

Gonzalez, Carmen G., 'Institutionalizing Inequality: The WTO Agreement on Agriculture, Food Security and Developing Countries', *Columbia Journal of International Law*, Vol. 27, No. 2, 2002, pp. 433–90.

Grier, Jen Heilman, 'Japan's Regulation of Large Retail Stores: Political Demands Versus Economic Interests', *University of Pennsylvania Journal of International Economic Law*, Vol. 22, 2001, pp. 1–60.

Grote, Ulrike, *Implications and Challenges of Liberalized Agricultural Markets for Developing Countries: An Institutional Perspective* (Bonn: Centre for Development Research, 2001).

Guasch, J. Luis, and Sarath Rajapatirana, *Antidumping and Competition Policies in Latin America and the Caribbean: Total Strangers or Soul Mates?*, World Bank Policy Research Working Paper No. 1958 (Washington, DC: World Bank, 1998).

Hainsworth, Susan, 'Sovereignty, Economic Integration and the World Trade Organization', *Osgoode Hall Law Journal*, Vol. 33, No. 3, 1995, pp. 584–622.

Hamilton, Carl B., and Will Martin, 'Introduction', in Carl Hamilton (ed.), *Textiles Trade and Developing Countries: Eliminating the Multi-Fibre Arrangement in the 1990s* (Washington, DC: World Bank, 1990), pp. 1–12.

Harris, Nigel, *The End of the Third World: Newly Industrialising Countries and the Decline of an Ideology* (Harmondsworth: Penguin Books, 1986).

Helms, Jesse, 'American Sovereignty and the UN', *The National Interest*, Vol. 62, Winter, 2000–01, pp. 31–4.

Hernandez-Lopez, Ernesto, 'Recent Trends and Perspectives for Non-State Actor Participation in World Trade Organization Disputes', *Journal of World Trade*, Vol. 35, 2001, pp. 469–98.

Higgott, Richard A., and Andrew Fenton Cooper, 'Middle Power Leadership and Coalition Building: Australia, the Cairns Group and the Uruguay Round of Trade Negotiations', *International Organization*, Vol. 44, No. 4, 1990, pp. 589–632.

Hindley, Brian, and Patrick Messerlin, *Antidumping Industrial Policy: Legalized Protection in the WTO and What to Do About It* (Washington, DC: American Enterprise Institute Press, 1996).

Ho, Yin-Ping, *Trade, Industrial Restructuring, and Development in Hong Kong* (London: Macmillan, 1992).

Hoekman, Bernard, *Reducing Agricultural Tariffs versus Domestic Support: What's More Important for Developing Countries*, World Bank Policy Research Working Paper No. 2918 (Washington, DC: World Bank, 2003).

Hoekman, Bernard and Michel Kostecki, *The Political Economy of the World Trading System: From GATT to WTO* (Oxford: Oxford University Press, 1995).

Holmes, Simon, 'Anti-circumvention under the European Union's New Anti-dumping Rules', *Journal of World Trade*, Vol. 29, No. 3, 1995, pp. 161–180.

Horlick, Gary N. and Eleanor C. Shea, 'The World Trade Organization Antidumping Agreement', *Journal of World Trade*, Vol. 29, No. 1, 1995, pp. 5–31.

Hudec, Robert E., 'The GATT Legal System: A Diplomat's Jurisprudence', *Journal of World Trade*, Vol. 4, No. 5, 1970, p. 615.

Hudec, Robert E., *Enforcing International Trade Law: The Evolution of the Modern GATT Legal System* (Salem, NH: Butterworth, 1993).

Hudec, Robert E., *Developing Countries in the GATT Legal System* (London: Gower for the Trade Policy Research Centre, 1987).

Ingco, Merlinda D. (ed.), *Agriculture, Trade and the WTO: Creating a Trading Environment of Development*, World Bank Policy Research Working Paper No. 418 (Washington, DC: World Bank, 2003).

Ingco, Merlinda D. and L. Alan Winters, *Agricultural Trade Liberalization in a New Trade Round: Perspectives of Developing Countries and Transition Economies*, World Bank Policy Research Working Paper No. 1271 (Washington, DC: World Bank, 2000).

Jackson, John H., 'The WTO "Constitution" and Proposed Reforms: Seven Mantras Revisited', *Journal of International Economic Law*, Vol. 4, No. 1, 2001, pp. 67–78.

Jackson, John H., 'The Perils of Globalization and the World Trading System', *Fordham Journal of International Law*, Vol. 24, Nos 1 and 2, 2000, pp. 371–82.

Jackson, John H., *The World Trade Organization: Constitution and Jurisprudence* (London: Royal Institute of International Affairs/Pinter, 1998).

Jackson, John H., 'The Great 1994 Sovereignty Debate: United States Acceptance and Implementation of the Uruguay Round Results', *Columbia Journal of Transnational Law*, Vol. 36, No. 1, 1997, pp. 157–88.

Jackson, John H., *The World Trading System: Law and Policy in International Economic Relations* (Cambridge, MA: MIT Press, 1989).

Jackson, John H., 'The Crumbling Institutions of the Liberal Trade System', *Journal of World Trade Law*, Vol. 12, No. 2, 1978, pp. 93–106.

Jennings, John M., 'In Search of a Standard: "Serious Damage" in the Agreement on Textiles and Clothing', *Northwestern Journal of International Law and Business*, Vol. 17, 1996, pp. 272–319.

Kaul, Tashi, 'The Elimination of Export Subsidies and the Future of Net Food-Importing Developing Countries in the WTO', *Fordham Journal of International Law*, Vol. 24, 2000, pp. 383–409.

Keesing, Donald B., *Improving Trade Policy Reviews in the World Trade Organization* (Washington, DC: Institute for International Economics, 1998).

Keohane, Robert, 'The Theory of Hegemonic Stability and Changes in International Economic Regimes', in Ole R. Holsti, Randolph M. Siverson and Alexander L. George (eds), *Change in the International System* (Boulder, CO: Westview Press, 1980).

Kerr, William A., 'The Next Step will be Harder: Issues for the New Round of Agricultural Negotiations at the World Trade Organization', *Journal of World Trade*, Vol. 34, 2000, pp. 123–40.

Kessie, Edwini, 'Enforceability of the Legal Provisions Relating to Special and Differential Treatment under the WTO Agreements', *Journal of World Intellectual Property*, Vol. 3, No. 6, 2000, pp. 955–75.

Kim, Jong Bum, 'Currency Conversion in the Anti-dumping Agreement', *Journal of World Trade*, Vol. 34, 2000, pp. 125–36.

Kindleberger, Charles P., *The World in Depression, 1929–1939* (Berkeley, CA: University of California Press, 1973).

Kisch, Herbert, *From Domestic Manufacture to Industrial Revolution: The Case of the Rhineland Textile Districts* (New York: Oxford University Press, 1989).

Koh, Harold Hongju, 'The Legal Markets of International Trade: A Perspective on the Proposed United States–Canada Free Trade Agreement', *Yale Journal of International Law*, Vol. 12, No. 2, 1987, pp. 193–249.

Krasner, Stephen, 'Structural Causes and Regime Consequences: Regimes as Intervening Variables', *International Organization*, Vol. 36, No. 2, 1982, pp. 185–205.

Krasner, Stephen, 'State Power and the Structure of International Trade', *World Politics*, Vol. 28, No. 3, 1976, pp. 317–47.

Krishna, Raj, *Antidumping in Law and Practice*, World Bank Policy Research Working Paper No. 1823, Washington, DC, 1997.

Krueger, Anne O., Developing Countries and the Next Round of Multilateral Trade Negotiations (Washington, DC: World Bank, 1999).

Krueger, Anne O., *Trade Policies and Developing Nations* (Washington, DC: Brookings Institution, 1995).

Kuczynski, Pedro-Pablo, and John Williamson (eds), *After the Washington Consensus: Restarting Growth and Reform in Latin America* (Washington, DC: Institute for International Economics, 2003).

Kufuor, Kofi Oteng, *The Growing Problem of Intra-LDC Antidumping Actions in World Trade* (University of East London: Eastlaw Press, 2001/2).

Kufuor, Kofi Oteng, 'The Developing Countries and the Shaping of the GATT/WTO Antidumping Code', *Journal of World Trade*, Vol. 32, No. 6, 1998, pp. 167–96.

Kufuor, Kofi Oteng, 'From the GATT to the WTO: The Developing Countries and the Reform of the Procedures for the Settlement of International Trade Disputes', *Journal of World Trade*, Vol. 31, No. 5, October 1997, pp. 117–47.

Kumar, Rajiv, 'Developing-Country Coalitions in International Trade Negotiations', in Diane Tussie and David Glover (eds), *The Developing Countries and World Trade: Policies and Bargaining Strategies* (Boulder, CO: Lynne Rienner, 1993), pp. 205–21.

Kuruvila, Pretty Elizabeth, 'Developing Countries and the GATT/WTO Dispute Settlement Mechanism', *Journal of World Trade*, Vol. 31, No. 6, 1997, pp. 171–208.

Kwon, Jene K., *The East Asian Model: An Exploration of Rapid Economic Growth in the Republic of Korean and Taiwan Province of China* (Geneva: United Nations Conference on Trade and Development, 1998).

Laird, Sam, 'The WTO's Trade Policy Review Mechanism: From Through the Looking Glass', *The World Economy*, Vol. 22, No. 6, August 1999, pp. 741–64.

Landau, Alice, 'Analyzing International Economic Negotiations: Towards a Synthesis of Approaches', *International Negotiation*, Vol. 5, No. 1, 2000, pp. 1–19.

Liebermann, Sima, *The Economic and Political Roots of the New Protectionism* (Lanham, MD: Rowman and Littlefield, 1988).

Lindseth, Peter L., 'Democratic Legitimacy and the Administrative Character of Supranationalism: The Example of the European Community', *Columbia Law Review*, Vol. 99, No. 3, 1999, pp. 628–738.

Long, Olivier, *Law and its Limitations in the GATT Multilateral Trade System* (Dordrecht, The Netherlands: Martinus Nijhoff, 1985).

Luke, David F., 'OAU/AEC Member States, the Seattle Preparatory Process and Seattle – A Personal Reflection', *Journal of World Trade*, Vol. 34, 2000, pp. 39–46.

Maas, Cynthia, 'Should the WTO Expand GATT Article XX? An Analysis of United States – Standards for Reformulated and Conventional Gasoline', *Minnesota Journal of Global Trade*, Vol. 5, 1996, pp. 415–39.

Macmillan, Fiona, *WTO and the Environment* (London: Sweet & Maxwell, 2001).

Malmgrem, Harold B., 'Trade Policy of Developed Countries for the Next Decade', in Jagdish N. Bhagwati (ed.), *The New International Economic Order: The North–South Debate* (Cambridge, MA: MIT Press, 1977), pp. 219–35.

Martin, Claude, 'The Relationship between Trade and Environment Regimes: What Needs to Change?', in Gary P. Sampson (ed.), *The Role of the World Trade Organization in Global Governance* (Tokyo: United Nations Press, 2001), pp. 137–54.

Martin, Will, and L. Alan Winters (eds.), *The Uruguay Round and the Developing Economies* (Washington, DC: The World Bank, 1995).

Mastel, Greg, *Antidumping Laws and the U.S. Economy* (Armonk, New York: M.E. Sharpe, 1998).

Matsushita, Mitsuo, Thomas J. Schoenbaum and Petros Mavriodis, *The World Trade Organization: Law, Practice and Policy* (Oxford: Oxford University Press, 2003).

Matthews, Alan, 'Developing Country Positions in WTO Agricultural Trade Negotiations', *Development Policy Review*, Vol. 20, No. 1, 2002, pp. 75–90.

Matthews, Alan, and Cathie Laroche-Dupraz, 'Agriculture Tariff Rate Quotas as a Development Instrument', *Trinity College Dublin Economic Papers* No. 2001/17, Dublin, Ireland, 2002.

Mavriodis, Petros C., 'Surveillance Schemes: The GATT's New Trade Policy Mechanism', *Michigan Journal of International Law*, Vol. 13, No. 2, 1992, pp. 374–414.

McGovern, Edmund, *International Trade Regulation: GATT, the United States and the European Community* (Exeter: Globefield Press, 1995).

McMahon, Joseph A., *Agricultural Trade, Protectionism and the Problems of Development* (Leicester: Leicester University Press, 1992).

McNeil, Ian R., 'Contracts: Adjustment of Long-Term Economic Relations under Classical, Neo-Classical and Relational Contract Law', *Northwestern University Law Review*, Vol. 72, No. 6, 1978, pp. 854–906.

McNutt, Patrick, *The Economics of Public Choice* (Cheltenham, UK: Edward Elgar, 2002).

McRae, Donald M., 'GATT Article XX and the WTO Appellate Body', in Marco Bronckers and Reinhard Quick (eds), *New Directions in International Economic Law: Essays in Honour of John H. Jackson* (The Hague: Kluwer Law International, 2000), pp. 219–36.

de Melo, Jaime, and L. Alan Winters, *Do Exporters Gain from Voluntary Export Restraints?*, World Bank Policy Research Working Paper No. 326 (Washington, DC: World Bank, 1990).

Messerlin, Patrick, 'Antidumping Laws and Developing Countries' (Washington, DC: World Bank, 1988).

Michalopolous, Constantine, *The Role of Special and Differential Treatment for Developing Countries in GATT and the World Trade Organization*, World Bank Policy Research Working Paper No. 2388 (Washington, DC: World Bank, 2000).

Michalopolous, Constantine, *Developing Country Participation in the WTO*, World Bank Policy Research Paper No. 1906 (Washington, DC: World Bank, 1998).

Moe, Terry M., 'Political Institutions: The Neglected Side of the Story', *Journal of Law, Economics and Organization*, special issue, Vol. 6, 1990, pp. 213–53.

Montana i Mora, Miguel, 'A GATT With Teeth: Law Wins Over Politics in the Resolution of International Trade Disputes', *Columbia Journal of Transnational Law*, Vol. 31, No. 1, 1993, pp. 103–80.

Moravcsik, Andrew, 'Taking Preferences Seriously: A Liberal Theory of International Politics', *International Organization*, Vol. 51, No. 4, 1997, pp. 513–53.

Morgenthau, Hans, *Politics among Nations: The Struggle for Power and Peace* (New York: Alfred A. Knopf, 1973).

Mukerji, Asoke, 'Developing Countries and the WTO: Issues of Implementation', *Journal of World Trade*, Vol. 34, 2000, pp. 33–74.

Nagle, John Charles, *Agricultural Trade Policies* (Farnborough: Saxon House, 1976).

Narlikar, Amritar, *International Trade and Developing Countries: Coalitions in GATT and WTO* (London: Routledge, 2003).

Neufeld, Inge Nora, *Anti-dumping and Countervailing Procedures: Use or Abuse? Implications for Developing Countries* (New York: UNCTAD, 2001).

Noland, Marcus, *Reconsidering the Washington Consensus: The Lessons from Asian Industrial Policy* (Washington, DC: International Institute for Development Economics, 2002).

North, Douglass C., *Institutions, Institutional Change and Economic Performance* (Cambridge: Cambridge University Press, 1990).

Odell, John, *Negotiating the World Economy* (Ithaca, New York: Cornell University Press, 2000).

Olsen, Jose Maria Figueres, Jose Manuel Salazar-Xirinachs and Monica Ara, 'Trade and Environment at the World Trade Organization: The Need for a Constructive Dialogue', in Gary P. Sampson (ed.), *The Role of the World Trade Organization in Global Governance* (Tokyo: United Nations University Press, 2001), pp. 155–82.

Olson, Mancur, *The Logic of Collective Action: Public Goods and the Theory of Groups* (Cambridge, MA: Harvard University Press, 1971).

Onyejekwe, Kele, 'GATT Agriculture and Developing Countries', *Hamline Law Review*, Vol. 17, 1993, pp. 77–153.

Page, Sheila, *Developing Countries in GATT/WTO Negotiations* (London: Overseas Development Institute, 2001).

Palmeter, David, 'A Commentary on the WTO Anti-Dumping Code', *Journal of World Trade*, Vol. 30, 1996, pp. 43–69.

Palmeter, David, and Petros C. Mavriodis, *Dispute Settlement in the World Trade Organization – Practice and Procedure* (The Hague, Netherlands: Kluwer Law International, 1999).

Park, Young-Il, and Kym Anderson, 'The Rise and Demise of Textiles and Clothing in Economic Development: The Case of Japan', in Michael Smitka (ed.), *The Textile Industry and the Rise of the Japanese Economy* (New York: Garland Publishing, 1998), pp. 165–82.

Patel, Chandrakant, *Single Undertaking: A Straitjacket or Variable Geometry* (Geneva: South Centre, 2003).

Perlow, Gary H., 'The Multilateral Supervision of International Trade: Has the Textiles Experiment Worked?', *American Journal of International Law*, Vol. 75, No. 1, 1981, pp. 93–133.

Pescatore, Pierre, William J. Davey and Andreas Lowenfeld (eds), *Handbook of GATT/WTO Dispute Settlement* (Irvington-on-Hudson, NY, and Transnational Publishers/The Hague: Kluwer Law International, 1996).

Petersmann, Ernst-Ulrich, *The GATT/WTO Dispute Settlement System: International Law, Organization and Dispute Settlement* (London: Kluwer Law International, 2 vols, 1997).

Preeg, Ernest H., *Traders in a Brave New World: The Uruguay Round and the Future of the International Trading System* (Chicago: University of Chicago Press, 1995).

Preeg, Ernest H., 'The US Leadership Role in World Trade: Past, Present and Future', *Washington Quarterly*, Vol. 15, No. 2, 1992, pp. 81–91.

Prusa, Thomas J., 'Why Are So Many Antidumping Petitions Withdrawn?', *Journal of International Economics*, Vol. 33, No. 1/2, 1992, pp. 1–20.

Puls, Bret, 'The Murky Waters of International Environmental Jurisprudence: A Critique of Recent WTO Holding in the Shrimp/Turtle Controversy', *Minnesota Journal of Global Trade*, Vol. 8, 1999, pp. 343–79.

Quick, Reinhard, 'The Community's Regulation on Leg-Hold Traps: Creative Unilateralism Made Compatible with WTO Law through Bilateral Negotiations?', in Marco Bronckers and Reinhard Quick (eds), *New Directions in International Economic Law: Essays in Honour of John H. Jackson* (The Hague: Kluwer Law International, 2000), pp. 237–57.

Raghavan, Chakravarthi, *Recolonization: GATT, Uruguay Round and the Third World* (London: Zed Books/Penang, Malaysia: Third World Network, 1990).

Ramsey, Robert, 'UNCTAD's Failures: The Rich Get Richer', *International Organization*, Vol. 38, No. 2, 1984, pp. 387–97.

Rege, Vinod, 'GATT Law and Environmentally-Related Issues Affecting the Trade of Developing Countries', *Journal of World Trade*, Vol. 28, 1994, pp. 95–169.

Reich, Arie, 'From Diplomacy to Law: The Juridicization of International Trade Relations', *Northwestern Journal of International Law and Business*, Vol. 17, No. 2/3,

1997, pp. 775–849.

Riaboi, Jorge B., 'Trade Liberalization and Dangerous Political Games', *Fordham International Law Journal*, Vol. 24, Nos 1 and 2, 2000, pp. 572–607.

Ricupero, Rubens, 'Rebuilding Confidence in the Multilateral Trading System: Closing the Legitimacy Gap', in Gary P. Sampson (ed.), *The Role of the World Trade Organization in Global Governance* (Tokyo: United Nations University, 2001), pp. 37–58.

Rom, Michael, *The Role of Tariff Quotas in Commercial Policy* (London: Macmillan, 1979).

Rusek, Christopher, 'Trade Liberalization in Developed Countries: Movement Toward Market Control of Agricultural Trade in the United States, Japan and the European Union', *Administrative Law Review*, Vol. 48, No. 2, 1996, pp. 493–513.

Sampson, Gary P., *Trade, Environment and the WTO: The Post-Seattle Agenda* (Washington, DC: Overseas Development Council, 2000).

Sapington, David E.M., 'Incentives in Principal-Agent Relationships', *Journal of Economic Perspectives*, Vol. 5, 1991, pp. 45–66.

Schaffer, Gregory C., 'The World Trade Organization under Challenge: Democracy and the Law and Politics of the WTO's Treatment of Trade and Environment Matters', *Harvard Environmental Law Review*, Vol. 25, No. 1, 2001, pp. 1–93.

van Schendelen, M.P.C.M., 'EC Committees: Influence Counts More Than Legal Powers', in Robin H. Pedler and Guenther F. Schaefer (eds), *Shaping European Law and Policy: The Role of Committees and Comitology in the Political Process* (Amsterdam: European Institute of Public Administration, 1996), pp. 25–37.

Scholte, Jan Aart, Robert O'Brien and Marc Williams, *The WTO and Civil Society* (Coventry: Centre for the Study of Globalisation and Regionalisation, University of Warwick, 1998).

Schultz, Jennifer, 'The GATT/WTO Committee on Trade and the Environment – Toward Environmental Reform', *American Journal of International Law*, Vol. 89, No. 2, 1995, pp. 423–39.

Shaw, Sabine, and Risa Schwarz, 'Trade and Environment in the WTO: State of Play', *Journal of World Trade*, Vol. 36, 2002, pp. 129–54.

Shukla, S.P., *From GATT to WTO and Beyond*, No. 195 (Helsinki: World Institute for Development Economics Research, United Nations University, 2000).

Simon, Herbert, 'A Behavioural Model of Rational Choice', *Quarterly Journal of Economics*, Vol. 69, No. 1, 1955, pp. 99–118.

Slaughter, Anne-Marie, 'Liberal International Relations Theory and International Economic Law', *The American University Journal of International Law and Policy*, Vol. 10, No. 2, 1995, pp. 717–43.

Smeets, Maarten, 'Main Features of the Uruguay Round Agreement on Textiles and Clothing, and Implications for the Trading System', *Journal of World Trade*, Vol. 29, No. 5, 1995, pp. 97–108.

Smith, Adam, *An Inquiry into the Nature and Causes of the Wealth of Nations*, 1776 (London: Everyman's Library, 1991).

Snidal, Duncan, 'Political Economy and International Institutions', *International Review of Law and Economics*, Vol. 16, No. 1, 1996, pp. 121–37.

Srinivasan, T.N., *Developing Countries and the Multilateral System: From the GATT to the Uruguay Round and the Future* (Boulder, CO: Westview Press, 1998).

Staffin, Elliot B., 'Trade Barrier or Trade Boon? A Critical Evaluation of Environmental Labelling and its Role in the "Greening" of World Trade', *Columbia Journal of Environmental Law*, Vol. 21, No. 2, 1996, pp. 205–86.

Stegemann, Klaus, *Price Undertakings to Settle Ani-Dumping Cases* (Montreal: Institute for Research on Public Policy, 1992).

Steinle, Jeffrey J., 'The Problem Child of World Trade: Reform School for Agriculture', *Minnesota Journal of Global Trade*, Vol. 4, No. 2, 1995, pp. 333–60.

Stewart, Terence P. (ed.), *The GATT Uruguay Round: A Negotiating History, 1986–1992* (Deventer, The Netherlands: Kluwer Law International, 1993).

Stewart, Terence P., Patrick J. McDonough and Marta M. Prando, 'Opportunities in the WTO for Increased Liberalization of Goods: Making Sure the Rules Work for All and that Special Needs are Addressed', *Fordham Journal of International Law*, Vol. 24, 2000, pp. 652–725.

Stiglitz, Joseph E., *More Instruments and Broader Goals: Moving Toward the Post-Washington Consensus* (Helsinki: World Institute for Development Economics Research, United Nations University, 1998).

Subedi, Surya P., 'Balancing International Trade with Environmental Protection: International Legal Aspects of Eco-Labels', *Brooklyn Journal of International Law*, Vol. 25, No. 2, 1999, pp. 373–405.

Summers, Clyde, 'The Battle in Seattle: Free Trade, Labour Rights, and Societal Values', *University of Pennsylvania Journal of International Economic Law*, Vol. 22, 2001, pp. 61–90.

Sung, Kim Fae, Kenneth A. Reinert and Chris G. Rodrigo, 'The Agreements on Textiles and Clothing: Safeguard Actions from 1995–2001', *Journal of International Economic Law*, Vol. 5, No. 2, 2002, pp. 445–68.

Tharakan, P.K.M., *The Problem of Anti-Dumping and Developing Country Exports* (Helsinki: World Institute for Development Economics Research, United Nations University, 2000).

Tharakan, P.K.M., 'The Political Economy of Anti-Dumping Undertakings in the European Communities', *European Economic Review*, Vol. 35, 1991, pp. 1341–59.

Tietje, Christian, 'Voluntary Eco-Labelling Programmes and Questions of State Responsibility in the WTO/GATT Legal System', *Journal of World Trade*, Vol. 29, 1995, pp. 123–58.

Trondal, Jarle, *Why Europeanisation Happens: The Transformative Power of EU Committees*, Arena Working Paper 02/3 (Oslo: Norwegian Institute for Studies in Research and Higher Education, 2002).

Tussie, Diane, *The Environment in International Trade Negotiations: Developing Country Stakes* (Basingstoke: Macmillan in association with the International Development Research Centre, Ottawa, 2000).

Tussie, Diane, *The Less Developed Countries and the World Trading System* (London: Pinter, 1987).

Tussie, Diane, and David Glover (eds), *The Developing Countries in World Trade: Policies and Bargaining Strategies* (Boulder, CO: Lynne Rienner, 1993).

Uchtmann, Donald L., Mary Osborn and Vince Maloney, 'Japanese Agriculture:

Tradition and the Modern Challenge', *Gonzaga Law Review*, Vol. 23, 1987–8, pp. 361–412.

Vaubel, Roland, 'A Public Choice View of International Organization', in Roland Vaubel and Thomas D. Willett (eds), *The Political Economy of International Organization: A Public Choice Approach* (Boulder, CO: Westview Press, 1991), pp. 27–45.

Verdirame, Gugliemo, 'The Definition of Developing Countries under GATT and other International Law', *German Yearbook of International Law*, Vol. 39, 1996, pp. 164–97.

Vermulst, Edwin, 'Anti-dumping in the Second Millennium: The Need to Revise Basic Concepts', in Marco Bronckers and Reinhard Quick (eds), *New Directions in International Economic Law: Essays in Honour of John H. Jackson* (The Hague: Kluwer Law International, 2000), pp. 259–78.

Viner, Jacob, *Dumping: A Problem in International Trade* (New York: Kelley, 1923).

Wallach, Lori, and Michelle Sforza, *Whose Trade Organization?: Corporate Globalization and the Erosion of Democracy: An Assessment of the World Trade Organization* (Washington, DC: Public Citizen, 1999).

Wangchuk, Sonam J., Michael Finger and Francis Ng, 'Antidumping as Safeguard Policy', (Washington, DC: World Bank, 2001).

Weston, A., *The Uruguay Round: Unravelling the Implications for the Least-Developed and Low-Income Countries* (Geneva: UNCTAD, 1994).

Whalley, John (ed.), *The Uruguay Round and Beyond: Final Report from the Ford Foundation Supported Project on Developing Countries and the Global Trading System* (London: Macmillan, 1989).

Williamson, John, 'What Should the World Bank Think about the Washington Consensus?', *World Bank Research Observer*, Vol. 15, No. 2, 2000, pp. 251–64.

Winham, Gilbert R., *International Trade and the Tokyo Round Negotiations* (Princeton, NJ: Princeton University Press, 1986).

Wolf, Martin, 'Why Voluntary Export Restraints?: An Historical Analysis', *The World Economy*, Vol. 12, 1989, pp. 273–91.

World Trade Organization, *The Legal Texts: The Results of the Uruguay Round of Multilateral Trade Negotiations* (Cambridge: Cambridge University Press, 1999).

Yano, Katsuyuki, 'Thirty Years of Being a Respondent in Antidumping Proceedings – Abuse of Economic Relief Can Have a Negative Impact on Competition Policy', *Journal of World Trade*, Vol. 33, No. 5, 1999, pp. 31–47.

Yarbrough, Beth V., and Robert M. Yarbrough, 'Institutions for the Governance of Opportunism in International Trade', *Journal of Law, Economics and Organization*, Vol. 3, No. 1, 1987, pp. 129–39.

Yusuf, A.A., *Legal Aspects of Trade Preferences for Developing States: a Study in the Influence of Development Needs on the Evolution of International Law* (Dordrecht, The Netherlands: Martinus Nijhoff, 1982).

Yusuf, A.A., 'Differential and More Favourable Treatment – the GATT Enabling Clause', *Journal of World Trade Law*, Vol. 14, 1980, pp. 488–507.

Zheng, Henry R., *Legal Structure of International Textile Trade* (New York: Quorum Books, 1988).

Zywicki, Todd J., *Baptists? The Political Economy of Political Environmental Interest Groups* (Arlington, VA: George Mason University, 2002).

SELECTED GATT/WTO DOCUMENTS

Annual Report – World Trade Organization (Geneva: World Trade Organization, various years).

Committee on Trade and Environment, Report of the Meeting Held on 24–25 July 1996.

Committee on Anti-Dumping Practices, Decision of 5 May 1980.

Committee on Anti-Dumping Practices, Decision of 20/22 October 1980.

Committee on Anti-Dumping Practices, Minutes of the Regular Meeting, 21–22 October 1996.

Committee on Anti-Dumping Practices, Minutes of the Regular Meeting, 28–29 April 1997.

Committee on Anti-Dumping Practices, Minutes of the Regular Meeting, 29 April 1999.

First Report of Committee II.

Fourth Report by the Committee on Anti-Dumping Practices.

Summary Report of the Meeting of the Ad Hoc Group on Implementation of the Committee on Anti-Dumping Practices, 29–30 April 1997.

Summary Report of the Meeting of the Ad Hoc Group on Implementation of the Committee on Anti-Dumping Practices, 22 October 1996.

Programme of Action Directed Towards an Expansion of International Trade, Decision of 17 November 1958.

Protocol Amending the General Agreement on Tariffs and Trade to Introduce a Part IV on Trade and Development, 1965.

Report by the Committee on Agriculture, 1996.

Report (2000), Textiles Monitoring Body.

Second Report of Committee III, 1959.

First Report of the Committee on Anti-Dumping Practices, 1970.

Second Report of the Committee on Anti-Dumping Practices, 1971.

Tenth Report of the Committee on Anti-Dumping Practices, 1978.

OTHER DOCUMENTS AND PUBLICATIONS

Agency for International Trade Information and Cooperation, 'Textiles and Clothing: Implications for Less-Advantaged Developing Countries', *http://www.acici.org/ aitic/ documents/Reports/report2ang.htm*.

Camdessus, Michel, 'Bolstering Market Access of Developing Countries in a Globalized World', *http://www.imf.org/external/np/speeches/1998/070698.htm*.

Economic Survey of Singapore (Singapore: Ministry of Trade and Industry, 1986).

FAO Technical Assistance and the Uruguay Round Agreements (Rome: Food and Agriculture Organization of the United Nations, 2nd edn, 1998).

The Multilateral Trade Agenda and the South (Geneva: The South Centre, 1998).

Oxfam GB, *Institutional Reform of the WTO* (Oxford: Oxfam, March 2000).

Reforming World Agricultural Trade: Policy Statement by Twenty-Nine Professionals from Seventeen Countries (Washington, DC: Institute for International Economics/ Ottawa, Canada: Institute for Research on Public Policy, 1988).

Bibliography

South Centre, *The Multilateral Trade Agenda and the South*, (Geneva: South Centre, 1998).

South Centre, 'The Future of the Group of 77', 28 April 1999, *http://www.sdnp.org.gy/minfor/sept99/future.html.*

United Nations Conference on Trade and Development, *Programme of Cooperation among Developing Countries, Exporters of Textiles and Clothing, Manual of Textile Negotiators* (Vol. 1, Geneva: UNCTAD, 1983).

US General Accounting Office, *International Trade: Use of the GATT Antidumping Code* (Washington, DC: US General Accounting Office, 1990).

United States International Trade Commission, *Potential Impact on the U.S. Economy and Industries of the GATT Uruguay Round Agreements* (Washington, DC: United States International Trade Commission, 1994).

United States International Trade Commission, *Review of the Effectiveness of Trade Dispute Settlement under the GATT and the Tokyo Round Agreements* (Washington, DC: United States International Trade Commission, 1985).

Index

Index

Index

Chatham House Papers

Global events move fast and Chatham House Papers respond with topical, accessible analysis of international affairs. Concise and lively, these books provide authoritative, informed and impartial comment for those with an interest in the world around them.

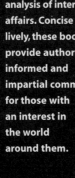

Vladimir Putin and the Evolution of Russian Foreign Policy == AVAILABLE

Bobo Lo
Royal Institute of International Affairs

"… the best overall assessment to date of Putin's foreign policy."
DR ALEX PRAVDA, ST ANTONY'S COLLEGE, OXFORD

"This is a Chatham House Paper at its best: the analysis is very well informed, the argument is succinct and persuasive and the presentation is accessible. Bobo Lo's examination of Russian foreign policy under Putin is the best work on the subject."
INTERNATIONAL AFFAIRS

March 2003 / 176 pages / 1-4051-0299-3 hb / 1-4051-0300-0 pb

Through the Paper Curtain == AVAILABLE

Insiders and Outsiders in the New Europe
Editors Julie Smith & Charles Jenkins
Royal Institute of International Affairs; Economist Intelligence Unit;

Eight central and east European states will join the European Union in 2004. Three of these states have already joined Nato; the rest will do so by 2004. This edited volume assesses the likely impact of EU and Nato enlargement on relations between these accession states and those destined to remain outside.

September 2003 / 224 pages / 1-4051-0293-4 hb / 1-4051-0294-2 pb

European Migration Policies in Flux == AVAILABLE

Changing Patterns of Inclusion and Exclusion
Christina Boswell
Royal Institute of International Affairs and Hamburg Institute of International Economics

"This outstanding book cuts in a lucid and accessible way to the core of the key migration policy dilemmas facing Europe. It will be an indispensable guide for anyone with an interest in these important questions."
ANDREW GEDDES, UNIVERSITY OF LIVERPOOL

September 2003 / 176 pages / 1-4051-0295-0 hb / 1-4051-0296-9 pb

America at War == FORTHCOMING

US Foreign Policy after 9/11
Michael Cox
London School of Economics

Argues that the global impact of 9/11 may be as significant as the changes brought about by the Cold War, and that US attempts to ensure a more secure world in an age of catastrophic terrorism may lead to even greater instability.

October 2004 / 200 pages / 1-4051-1986-1 hb /1-4051-1985-3 pb

Forthcoming books in the series

Exit the Dragon?
Privatization and State Control in China
Editors Stephen Green & Guy Liu Shaojia

The New Atlanticist
Poland's Foreign and Security Priorities
Kerry Longhurst & Marcin Zaborowski

Putin's Russia and the Wider Europe
Roy Allison, Margot Light & Stephen White

Blackwell
Publishing